THE DAREDEVIL'S MANUAL

THE DAREDEVIL'S MANUAL

HOW TO PARACHUTE OFF A BUILDING,
WALK ON HOT COALS,
EAT A LIVE SCORPION,
SWALLOW A SWORD,
AND DOZENS OF OTHER THINGS
THAT PROFESSIONAL DAREDEVILS DO

BEN IKENSON
ILLUSTRATIONS BY JEROME BECKLEY

BARNES & NOBLE BOOKS
NEW YORK

This edition published by Barnes & Noble, Inc.,
by arrangement with EYE Quarto, Inc.

2004 Barnes & Noble Books

Text copyright © 2004 EYE Quarto, Inc.

Illustrations copyright © 2004 EYE Quarto, Inc.

M 10 9 8 7 6 5 4 3 2 1

ISBN 07607-5644-9

Conceived, designed, and produced by EYE.

Managing Editor: Michael Driscoll
Editor: Reeve Chace
Cover/Interior designer: Gary Cravener Design
Copy editors: Jane Elias and Stephanie Finnegan
Proofreaders: Edwin Kiester, Jr. and Adam Sommers

Publisher: William Kiester

Library of Congress Cataloging-in-Publication Data on file.

Printed in China.

WARNING

The descriptions of activities, stunts, and feats of derring-do in this book are for ENTERTAINMENT PURPOSES ONLY. We do not advise or recommend you attempt any of the activities described herein. Much of the information in this book comes from highly skilled and experienced daredevils. By presenting the descriptions and information herein, we make no representation that the information is safe, accurate, or appropriate for the activities described. The daredevils, author, and publishers hereby specifically disclaim any liability, loss, or risk for harm to any person or property resulting from (directly or indirectly) the use, misuse, or application of any description or information in this book and are not engaged in rendering any advice or instruction with respect to any of the subject matter contained herein. The information provided herein should not be construed or interpreted to encourage, advocate, condone, or permit the violation of any civil or criminal law or regulation of any country, state, province, municipality, or local government. We urge you to act in conformity with the personal, pecuniary, and property rights of all other persons and entities.

ACKNOWLEDGMENTS

Many thanks to EYE and Will Kiester for daring me to undertake this project. Like the trusty assistants who aid the daredevils depicted in the pages, editors Michael Driscoll and Reeve Chace prodded me graciously along, right over the edge, helping to execute the dare with precision and panache. They combine the keen eyes of superbly talented editors with the flair of gifted creative writers.

I am profoundly grateful to my good friend, veteran journalist, author and radio talk show host Dennis Domrzalski. This book would simply not have been possible without his expertise, professionalism and commitment. During the project, he provided invaluable research and conducted many of the interviews on which the book is largely based. He was tireless in uncovering the truth behind the dare. He happens to be a certifiably insane daredevil who has been known to take long-distance motorcycle trips in sub-freezing temperatures with insufficient protection against the elements. I suppose in dealing with this project, he was not on all too unfamiliar ground.

Thanks for the good references and insider information from carnival historian James Taylor, and from performance artist Harley Newman, both of whom are featured in the book.

Thanks especially to all the daredevils who contributed their expertise and who in doing the daring things they do provided for this book's conception.

Thanks to my parents who dared provide for the author's conception.

Thanks to my lovely lady friend Melanie Ruiz: She's the safety net to my tightrope walk; the parachute to my freefall; the Knievel to my Evel.

—Ben Ikenson

TABLE OF CONTENTS

I. AMAZING ANATOMY

II. STRENGTH, DEXTERITY, AND BALANCE

III. TAMING THE WILD BEAST

IV. THE RAZOR'S EDGE

V. MOTORHEADED MADNESS

VI. FLIGHTS OF FANCY

CAUTION:
THIS BOOK MAY BE HAZARDOUS TO YOUR HEALTH

This book may be hazardous to your health if misinterpreted. This book is not intended to offer actual instruction. Rather, its educational value lies in its offering of unique insight into the daredevil's world and descriptions of some—not all—of the technical skills and artistry by which the daredevil masters his particular craft. While I have enjoyed learning about how the stunts described herein are performed, I did not gather enough information to safely replicate them. While many of these stunts are technically possible to learn, they are also inherently—and extremely—dangerous. Attempting any one of them can result in serious injury and/or death. This book's intention is merely to outline how professional daredevils do what they do, without dying. Attempting what these experts have mastered over years of training and development of specialized skills is, in no uncertain terms, to dramatically increase your risk of death.

—Ben Ikenson

INTRODUCTION: SYMPATHY FOR THE DAREDEVIL

On October 25, 1975, in King's Island, Ohio, Robert Craig "Evel" Knievel prepared to attempt a motorcycle jump over fourteen Greyhound buses. The tension was almost unbearable: Just a few months prior, Knievel had made an attempt to clear thirteen double-decker buses in the packed Wembley Stadium in London. But on that day, he hit the top of the last bus and tumbled violently, coming to a final halt with his Harley-Davidson on top of him. He suffered a broken hand, a broken pelvis, and a concussion. He also made a famous declaration: "I will never, ever jump again. I am through."

Of course, this turned out to be untrue. Ever defiant, Knievel was back on his bike three months later, preparing for the stunt in Ohio. It was this attitude that made Evel Knievel a legend. With his over-the-top outfits (he often wore red, white, and blue jumpsuits with billowing capes) and his outrageous, death-defying stunts, his was a rare brew of showmanship and intoxicating suspense.

Years later, wide-eyed, my brothers and I watched television rebroadcasts of the stunt, Knievel launching himself over those fourteen Greyhounds. Even the rerun of his historic stunt, with its predetermined outcome, held us captive. The moment he flew off that ramp, as the television flickered and Knievel hung in the air, time stood still. When he landed, unscathed, we all breathed a quick sigh of relief and then hooted ecstatically. Arguments would later ensue as to who got to be Evel Knievel for Halloween.

Like most people, my brothers and I were mired in everyday rules: common sense, gravity, physics, and a fear of danger. However, the daredevil on the bike, who seemed to defy all conventions, momentarily liberated us from these down-to-earth concerns. Therein lies the daredevil's attraction: he not only breaks the rules, he rewrites them.

Mass media helped Evel Knievel open the daredevil's world to a wider audience. Feats of danger and daring, however, have fascinated spectators for ages. Harry Houdini brought acts of magic and suspense to the people a century ago, in the early

1900s. Before that, bicyclists took the "leap for life" over ramps in the big top's center ring, men went over Niagara Falls in barrels, and Blondin—grandest wire walker of his time—took to the high wire with a full stove-and-kitchen setup, cooking himself breakfast in midair.

Part showman, part shaman, the daredevil is as old as the Devil himself. Many of the exploits featured in this book originate in ancient India and the Middle East, where elite spiritualists performed mind-boggling feats that spoke to the strength of the human will and a seemingly supernatural mental acumen. Some of the oldest stunts known include sword swallowing, walking over hot coals, and hammering nails into one's own face, incredible displays that are still performed today.

The modern descendants of these early spiritualists are today's biker babes and madmen motorcyclists, brick-breaking and karate-chopping Christian missionaries, knife-chucking reverends, bearded ladies whose five o'clock shadows buzz and sting, and contortionists who squeeze into small boxes, among many others. I selected the subjects featured here by first pursuing the most recognizable, most celebrated, most spectacular stunts I'd witnessed through years of marveling at daredevils. One stunt led to another, and soon the collection you see here took shape. These daredevils range from the comically twisted to the borderline insane. But all of them bring a unique sense of character to the stunts they perform. And all were extraordinarily generous in revealing the secrets behind their skills.

While the range of daring acts is broad and diverse, the result is often the same: cathartic. The daredevil, by definition and virtue, amuses and amazes; the daredevil gives an expression to absurdity and a voice to the inane; the daredevil makes science of senselessness and stretches human boundaries. Or, like Evel Knievel, the daredevil has a special ability to freeze a moment into a small eternity, while those of us in the time warp marvel at the execution.

—Ben Ikenson

I.

AMAZING ANATOMY

Chapter 1

EATING FIFTY HOT DOGS IN TWELVE MINUTES

Despite a modern-day global epidemic of obesity, the world of competitive speed eating is only growing larger. But in competitions, a heavyweight may not be so great. At the 2002 Nathan's Famous Fourth of July International Hot Dog Eating Contest, a diminutive 140-pound Japanese man named Takeru Kobayashi took the crown—or rather, the mustard-yellow international belt. He also set a world record by downing fifty and a half hot dogs and buns during the twelve-minute duration of the contest.

YIELD
TO COMMON
SENSE

COMPETITIVE SPEED EATING CAPITAL

The world of competitive speed eating is as strange and diverse as the menu items on the planet: There are cannoli-eating contests, matzo ball–gobbling standoffs, and even pomme frites–consuming competitions. Apparently, while other skills may fail to impress, the ability to eat large quantities in short amounts of time holds serious global currency.

In this culture, one crown remains the most coveted. The annual Nathan's Famous Fourth of July International Hot Dog Eating Contest in New York City is, bar none, the Super Bowl of competitive speed eating—no less important than the World Cup is to football/soccer enthusiasts. New York's Coney Island, where the first Nathan's Famous restaurant opened, has been the stage for the annual competition since 1916. The event marries that competitive spirit of the early Greek Olympics with the gluttony of ancient Rome.

"I take care of my stomach and I like to talk to it," Kobayashi said at the time. Eating healthy and staying

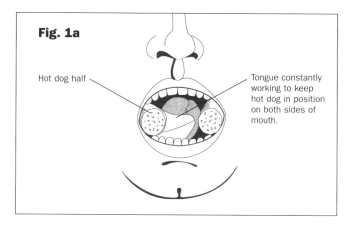

Fig. 1a

Hot dog half

Tongue constantly working to keep hot dog in position on both sides of mouth.

regular are two of the main tricks that neophyte competitive eaters often overlook. The stomach should be in excellent shape to efficiently endure the abuse it receives during competition. The night before competing, consider eating a large amount of roughage, which can help vacate the bowels to leave room for the next occupant—in this case, an inordinate amount of processed meat product.

Kobayashi breaks his wieners in two and alternates bites from both halves into his mouth, capitalizing on the speed of two hands to deliver the food almost robotically to his face. Top eaters like Kobayashi take strategic bites of food that are as large as they can comfortably swallow. According to an article about speed eating in the *New York Times*, the most efficient eaters are able to "relax the upper esophageal sphincter, overriding the gag reflex." Moistening the bun, as Kobayashi does, helps conserve precious saliva and digestive fluids.

HOW THE DAREDEVIL DOES IT

These instructions are for reading entertainment only. They are not to be followed, nor do they convey the full extent of knowledge and training required to attempt these dangerous acts.

Checklist: 50 hot dogs; 50 buns; 1 stopwatch; 1 bowl of water

1. Drink a precontest shot of cooking oil (linseed or olive) to lubricate the esophagus for smoother and speedier swallowing.

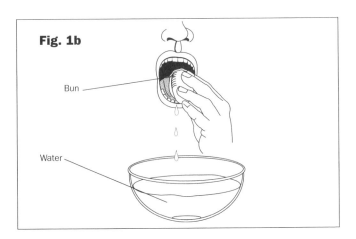

Fig. 1b

Bun

Water

2. Once the starting bell rings, separate the hot dogs from the buns.

3. Select a hot dog and break it in half.

4. Take strategically sized bites from both halves of the hot dog. Always chew two separate morsels of food simultaneously, one on each side of the mouth. Use the tongue to keep the food in line with your bite (see Fig. 1a).

5. Swallow the largest bites possible. (Time is of the essence, and chewing eats up the clock.)

6. Select a bun and soak it in the bowl of water.

7. Break the bun up and squeeze it into small balls.

8. Swallow bun balls whole (see Fig. 1b).

9. Repeat steps 3 through 8 fifty times in twelve minutes.

DANGER: Rapid-paced overeating can lead to heartburn, bellyache, and excruciating nausea; habitual overeating can lead to morbid obesity, a major health concern.

Chapter 2

SUCKING SPAGHETTI INTO THE MOUTH AND BLOWING IT OUT THE NOSE

O n December 16, 1998, twenty-four-year-old Kevin Cole of Carlsbad, New Mexico, earned a place in the *Guinness Book of World Records* when he blew a seven-and-a-half-inch strand of spaghetti out of his nose to a record distance of seven and a half inches. Cole has also demonstrated his remarkable skill at sucking one end of spaghetti up one nostril and blowing it out the other, achieving what has been called the "nasal floss" effect.

"SPAGHETTI WESTERNER"

Though not well documented, the spaghetti-through-the-nose trick is one of the most unusual anatomical stunts, if not for its pure entertainment value, then for its defiance of the laws of human physiology. It blurs the line between the processes of breathing and eating in an entertainingly disgusting way.

How to note such remarkable achievements on a résumé may be an even bigger challenge for the young man. But if hometown loyalty is considered a plus to potential employers, he needn't worry. "It's not very often that Carlsbad gets put on the map like this," Cole told reporters.

Cole still holds his record, and a noteworthy job. An EMT

and firefighter in his hometown, Cole got interested in performing the spaghetti stunt not long before he earned his record. "While I was underwater once, I had my mouth full of water and I sneezed. When all the water came rushing out my nose, it dawned on me that I could shoot stuff through my nose. Later, I was watching the previous record holder do his thing on TV. That very night, my wife happened to be making ramen and so I tried it, it worked, and I beat his distance that very first time. I immediately called Guinness and was instructed to make a videotape of the stunt. Two weeks later I was on a plane to California for the Guinness world record prime-time TV show."

Cole adds boldly: "And if somebody wants to challenge the champ, I'm ready!" But he offers a very straightforward warning: "Be careful, because you're putting a foreign object into your air valve."

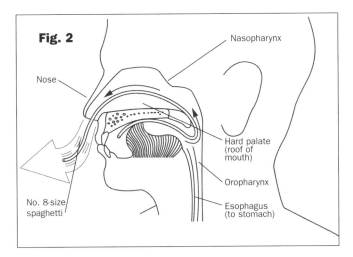

Fig. 2

Nasopharynx

Nose

Hard palate (roof of mouth)

Oropharynx

No. 8-size spaghetti

Esophagus (to stomach)

HOW THE DAREDEVIL DOES IT

These instructions are for reading entertainment only. They are not to be followed, nor do they convey the full extent of knowledge and training required to attempt these dangerous acts.

Checklist: no. 8-size spaghetti; olive oil; clear nasal

1. Cook spaghetti. Use a dab of olive oil in the boiling water but no salt. (Do not overcook or

spaghetti will not be strong enough to withstand the force of your sharp exhale.) Strain noodles and wait until they are at room temperature.

2. Suck a spaghetti strand into your mouth, holding one end with an index finger and a thumb.

3. Let the noodle slide to the back of your throat, but keep it pushed up with the back of your tongue.

4. Let the tip of your tongue take the end of the noodle from your hand and clamp it to the roof of your mouth. The farther back along the roof of your mouth that the front tip of the noodle is clamped, the more power you will have for ejection.

5. Once the strand is secure, take a deep breath.

6. Cover one nostril with a finger.

7. Force the air out of your lungs through your nostril while releasing your tongue's grip on the end of the spaghetti strand (see Fig. 2).

NASAL FLOSS

For the "nasal floss" effect, hold the noodle in place with your tongue while you push the air out of your lungs. With the noodle then dangling out of one nostril, place a finger over that nostril to hold the strand in place, and to cut off airflow. Maneuver the tip of the noodle in your mouth toward the back of your oral cavity, prop it up with the back of your tongue, then repeat air thrust through the empty nostril.

DANGER: If the entire spaghetti strand isn't ejected, pasta particles may lodge in the larynx or trachea. This can lead to infection and erosion of the voice box.

SUCKING SPAGHETTI INTO THE MOUTH AND BLOWING IT OUT THE NOSE

Chapter 3

BURPING AT OVER ONE HUNDRED DECIBELS

Burping is universal and means many things. You've eaten well; you've drunk a beer or four; you're practicing a stunt that will most likely gross out anybody within earshot. That's the reaction twenty-two-year-old Jon Oesch noticed, without too much concern, on an airline flight from his home in Detroit, Michigan, to Los Angeles, California, for a burping contest. "Flight attendants and fellow passengers were disgusted by my constant burping, but, hey, I had to practice!"

EXCUSE ME!

In 1976, the Who played the loudest concert ever: 67,000 watts rocked the venue at 125 decibels, earning the band a place in The *Guinness Book of World Records*. A generation later, a fellow Englishman followed suit with another high-volume triumph for the United Kingdom. On April 5, 2000, judges conferred a new world record when thirty-one-year-old Londoner Paul Hunn unleashed a 118.1-decibel belch—the loudest burp known to history and humankind. His thunderous accomplishment has been compared to the volume of a jumbo jet taking off from only one hundred yards away.

Of course, where he was bound would only disgust people even more. "In L.A.," says Oesch, "it was even more fun as the four to five people who were to be in the contest were put up at the same hotel. We hung out together, went to restaurants, movies and malls, and we were burping all the time. The maids looked disgusted. Everywhere we went, we were burping."

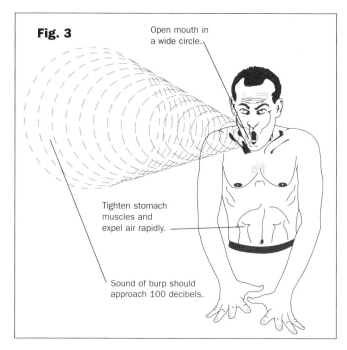

Fig. 3

Open mouth in a wide circle.

Tighten stomach muscles and expel air rapidly.

Sound of burp should approach 100 decibels.

Oesch won the contest, but only held the world's record of burping at 115 decibels—the volume of rifle fire—for a brief time, until his record was usurped by Paul Hunn. However, Oesch says he's been promised a burp-off against Hunn.

The talent for burping at high decibels is not an accomplishment that is achieved, at first, on purpose. Oesch began burping loudly in the first grade. He realized he had something when classmates began laughing. Today, he says, he can burp all day long and never get a sick stomach. He also says he can burp constantly without harming himself.

But it was not until much later that he realized his talent could bring fame beyond the attention of his friends and family. "The first time I really found out I was good at it, I was a camp counselor for the YMCA in high school and went to the Michigan state fair in 1998 at Davisburg," says Oesch. "I competed in a burping contest and I won easily."

The next thing he knew, he was being written up in local papers, and soon after, The *Guinness Book of World Records* called him and sent him airfare to Los Angeles for the burping contest.

Oesch offers insight on how he does it: "You swallow air. Some people drink stuff like soda (for the carbonation). I don't do anything special. I just keep swallowing air until my stomach bloats. I push the air down with my tongue. I don't know how to explain it. It's kind of weird."

Before doing the big burp, Oesch takes between twenty and thirty swallows of air. He keeps swallowing air until "I feel like I'm going to explode," he says. "Then I tighten up my stomach like I'm going to take a punch to the stomach and then I just let it all out at once. The faster you push the air out, the louder burp you get."

How exactly Oesch gets his burps so loud, even he cannot say for sure, although it might have something to do with the amount of air pressure he is able to build up in his stomach. Why does a balloon pop when you prick it? Because of  the pressurized air inside; a gas under great pressure makes a loud noise when it is suddenly released. Oesch's anatomy is apparently specially equipped to amplify the explosion of gas from his stomach. Oesch is just one of those rare individuals blessed with the ability to make people turn around and say, "Well, excuuuuuu-use me!"

HOW THE DAREDEVIL DOES IT

These instructions are for reading entertainment only. They are not to be followed, nor do they convey the full extent of knowledge and training required to attempt these dangerous acts.

Checklist: nothing but air

1. While standing straight, fill your stomach with air by gulping down between twenty and thirty large breaths.

2. Hold the air in your stomach.

3. Tighten your stomach as if you are about to receive a punch.

4. Open your mouth in a wide circle and push the air out: The faster you push the air out, the louder burp you get (see Fig. 3).

5. Say, "Excuse me."

DANGER: Burping at high volumes poses more danger to your ears than to your internal organs. Sounds above 85 decibels may induce hearing loss in anyone exposed to the noise. Also, subjecting others to your own high-volume belching may trigger negative and potentially violent responses from those within earshot.

Chapter 4

SQUIRTING MILK OUT OF THE EYE

Mike Moraal was able to silence talk-show host David Letterman briefly after appearing on his show for a segment on stupid human tricks. "Letterman was hard-pressed for words after I performed—usually he has some witty response, but he just stood there in awe with mouth agape."

LACTOSE EYE-TOLERANT

The ability to squirt milk out of one's eye comes with a variety of hidden benefits: you can discourage annoying neighbors from stopping by for coffee if they see how you add the cream, or you can upstage the astronaut on your child's Bring Your Parent to Class Day.

Thirty-four-year-old Moraal, of Vancouver, British Columbia, Canada, has been squirting milk out of his eye socket for the past ten years. In fact, in 2001, he milked his eye on French television for a world-record distance of 103 inches. In addition to David Letterman's program and France's *L'Émission des Records,* Moraal has appeared on the *Guinness Book of World Records* TV show, London's *The Word,* Germany's *Gottschalk Late Night, Penn & Teller in Las Vegas, Whose Line Is It Anyway?* and Steve Harvey's *Big Time Show.*

But not so long ago, Moraal was an anonymous student and restaurant employee. "I discovered I could do this during my employment at a steakhouse," he says. "I was putting myself through art school and worked the weekends to help offset the cost of my schooling. A patron asked me to bring him a raw egg in a glass. He was

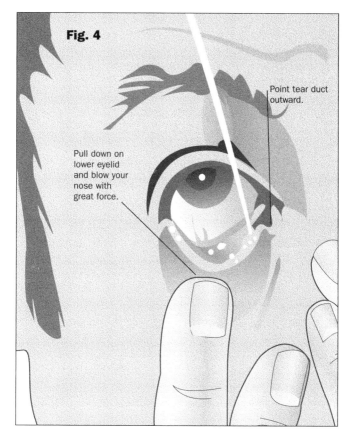

Fig. 4

Point tear duct outward.

Pull down on lower eyelid and blow your nose with great force.

going to settle a bet with some of his buddies. Well, he takes the egg up his nose, yolk and all, and swallows it down his throat. Pretty impressive, I thought at the time."

And so, one good thing leads to another.

"Well, the next night I was with my brother Rick and a few friends," Moraal says. "I thought I'd give it a try. Good for a laugh, I thought. Well, in the middle of the trick I feel an enormous sneeze coming on. I didn't want to have egg spew all over the place so I held my nose tightly and sneezed, and from my eye, egg flew through the air, in what seemed to be slow motion, and landed in the dead center of the table. Everyone's watching this yellow blob flying through the air, and as soon as it land-ed on the table, all the guys began to howl. They could not believe what they had seen. So I started experiment-ing with various fluids and techniques and it evolved into my finely tuned act."

From the chance spectacle of a raw-egg-snorting restau-rant patron, a world-class eye-socket milk squirter was born. Curious about his talent, Moraal approached the University of Oregon's optometry department, and there he learned about his faulty valve.

"Apparently," Moraal says, "there is a valve in your nose [that] is normally meant to drain fluids, such as tears, down your throat. For most people this valve works in one direction—for me it works both ways. I am able to force fluids back up through this valve. Once the fluid is forced through the valve, it gets stored in a pouch or eye sac regularly reserved for storing tears. At this point, I plug my nose and blow as though I'm attempting to clear my nose. The pressure builds up, and air is forced up through my faulty valve, and forces the fluids from the eye sac out its only escape—the tear duct."

If you, too, have a faulty valve in your nose, you may be able to squirt milk out your eye.

HOW THE DAREDEVIL DOES IT

These instructions are for reading entertainment only. They are not to be followed, nor do they convey the full extent of knowledge and training required to attempt these dangerous acts.

Checklist: shot of milk; faulty eye valve

1. Fill a shot glass with milk—skim, 2 percent, or whole, whatever you prefer.

2. While plugging one nostril with your finger, snort the milk up the other nostril.

3. Once the milk has filled your nasal cavity, plug that nostril by pressing your finger against the outside of the nostril.

4. Pull down on the lower eyelid closest to the nostril with the milk in it, pointing the tear duct outward.

5. With great force, blow as if you're trying to clear your nose. If you have a faulty valve, the milk will come out through your tear duct (see Fig. 4).

DANGER: It is generally an unwise idea to put foreign substances in your nasal cavities. In particular, milk can host various bacteria that, if lodged in your head, may cause serious illness and potentially irreversible tissue decay.

Chapter 5

HAMMERING A NAIL INTO THE FACE

Erik Sprague, aka the Lizardman, is a sideshow stunt performer whose skills and lizardlike body modifications (including tattoos of green scales, surgically created horned ridges above his eyes, and a surgically altered forked tongue) make for both a memorable showman and a memorable act: he swallows swords; he walks on broken glass (see page 112); he lifts weights hung from piercings in his nipples; and, yes, he performs his own version of the ancient human blockhead stunt, which he dubs the Lizard Blockhead.

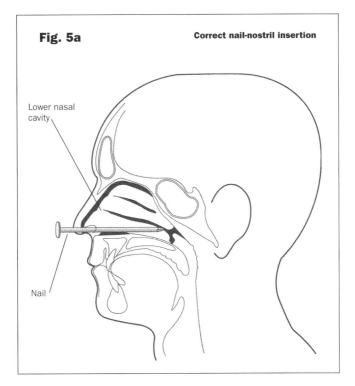

Fig. 5a

Correct nail-nostril insertion

Lower nasal cavity

Nail

HUMAN BLOCKHEAD

After sword swallowing, the nail-in-the-face trick is one of the oldest stunts in history. It was a regular yogic feat of the fakirs, the street-performing spiritualists of ancient India and the Middle East. Europeans imported the stunt—sometimes along with the fakir who performed it—to provide novel entertainment to audiences who were simultaneously amazed and repulsed. It was circus sideshow legend Melvin Burkhart who popularized and performed the stunt throughout much of the twentieth century. Burkhart named it the "Human Blockhead," and the name has stuck ever since.

"Actually," Sprague says, "it's not horribly physically challenging but it takes work to make it an interesting presentation, and it takes a pretty good knowledge of your own anatomy."

In the human nostril there are two passages that travel from the face into the skull. One goes up vertically, and

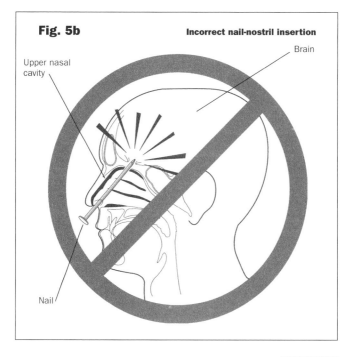

Fig. 5b

Incorrect nail-nostril insertion

Brain

Upper nasal cavity

Nail

NOSING AROUND

Cotton swabs are good to practice with, according to Sprague, because they are relatively clean. One of the more serious dangers of prying around deep within your nasal cavity is the potential to scrape or nick yourself in an area that is both hard to access and close to the brain. "A little scratch can easily become a life-threatening infection," Sprague says.

one goes straight back. "Don't go up!" Sprague warns. That road is dangerous and painful. The other passage leads to the back of the throat. To find it, Sprague recommends using a cotton swab. "With firm grip, feel around," he says. "The passage narrows, but then it opens towards the back. But maintain a firm grip on the cotton swab. You don't want to have to go to an emergency room scrambling for excuses as to how such an object got stuck in your nose."

One of the initial challenges in preparing for the stunt is conditioning the sneeze reflex. If you feel yourself about to sneeze, remove the object quickly but carefully. The head contains an interconnected system of ear and nasal canals and tear ducts; envision sneezing while pinching your nose shut and you can imagine the potential danger and discomfort of sneezing while an object is blocking your nasal passages. The point is to understand your body's responses, and after conditioning the responses, move up to wider objects, such as three cotton swabs at a time, as Sprague suggests.

SANE PEOPLE
**KEEP
RIGHT**
OF THIS STUNT

Once you are ready for the real deal, you should know the length of your nasal passage: most are about four and a half to five inches long. Use a nail that conforms to this length, perhaps a quarter of an inch or so shorter. "You do not want to tap something that can hit and puncture the lower sinus cavity, which is basically the bottom of the brain pan," Sprague says (see Fig. 5a).

The sinus area is very sensitive, and you will feel it when the nail gets close. Also consider using a nail with a large enough head to prevent it from entering the nostril interior.

HOW THE DAREDEVIL DOES IT

These instructions are for reading entertainment only. They are not to be followed, nor do they convey the full extent of knowledge and training required to attempt these dangerous acts.

Checklist: a sterilized nail; a mean-looking claw hammer

1. Clean the nail well and file its point to smooth edges, or use a custom-made nail for a "showier" look. Some specialty and magic shops sell nails specifically for this purpose.

2. Tilt your head back to about a thirty-degree angle. Slide the nail into the opening of the lower nasal cavity, keeping a firm grip on the nail.

3. Using a hammer, lightly tap the nail deeper into the nasal cavity.

4. Once you feel the tip of the nail approach the back of the lower sinus cavity, stop tapping (see Fig. 5b). Show your audience that the nail is almost completely impaled in your face.

5. Turn the hammer around, smoothly slide the nail out by using the hammer's claw, and take a bow.

DANGER: Obstructing the nasal passage with foreign objects yields many potential hazards, including serious infection and undue strain on other sensitive passageways within the head.

HAMMERING A NAIL INTO THE FACE

Chapter 6

SKEWERING A BICEPS

orty-year-old Tim Cridland is better known as Zamora the Torture King for his pain-defying performances. He has enjoyed more than a decade in the circus sideshow biz, and now, every weekend in Las Vegas, he puts on a show called "Shock!" Of course, his interest began long before he was lured by neon lights.

ARM KABOB

If you are afraid of needles, skewers will hold even less appeal for you. Not for the faint of heart, nor the wary of wounding, this stunt can be a real pain in the arm! But when performed correctly, it can be a relatively pain-free feat of mind over matter. The matter, in this case your anatomy, must be studied very carefully, and the mind requires its own schooling.

The son of a botany professor, Zamora grew up in the small town of Pullman, Washington, where, until his mid-twenties, he did odd manual-labor jobs, including operating a movie theater projector. As he grew up, though, he began developing an interest in circus stunts—and torture in particular.

"I read about the stuff in a book that had people from all over the world doing strange acts—people doing snake swallowing, walking on hot coals. I thought it was pretty interesting," says Zamora. "I also saw shows like *That's Incredible!* I grew up in a small town, and, of course, I would never see anything like that [in my real life]. We had a circus come through and I saw it and I had a pent-up interest and I kept learning more and more about it over many, many years. I learned to eat fire when I was eighteen or nineteen. I got some books on it and I got

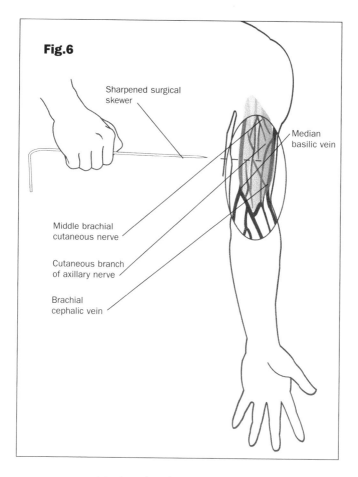

Fig.6

Sharpened surgical skewer

Median basilic vein

Middle brachial cutaneous nerve

Cutaneous branch of axillary nerve

Brachial cephalic vein

some personal instruction from a youth circus in the Northwest."

One thing led to the next and by the early 1990s Zamora was touring with the music festival Lollapalooza, which garnered him national recognition. "A lot of this circus stuff and sideshow acts had died down," Zamora says, "but right about then, interest began to pick up. It was good timing and I got in at the right moment. This is much more thrilling and interesting than doing any type of normal job."

Zamora is fascinated with Eastern culture and incorporates that into his show. "I'm continually trying to resurrect feats from the past or from other cultures—stuff that isn't available in Western culture," he says.

Hence, the human shish kebab: Zamora pierces himself with a surgical fourteen-to-sixteen-gauge nonporous metal skewer that measures six to eight inches long, an instrument normally used for setting broken bones. He sharpens it at one end.

"I sterilize them and I reuse them," he says. "I'm very relaxed when I do it. I go right through the muscle. I can flex my muscle when it is in and that can bend the skewer.

"I had to get the knowledge from photos and from anatomy books. You have to see where to go to avoid the major arteries and go on top or under the nerve bundles. You have to find a very specific place. I have to be very precise on where I'm going through."

The skewer punctures a hole in his skin, but Zamora says he rarely bleeds when he does the stunt. He pierces himself in different places to keep from repeatedly hitting the same spot, which can create scar tissue and make it harder to break through the skin, he says. He sometimes does five skewering shows a day.

Surprisingly, Zamora didn't practice much before attempting the stunt in front of an audience for the first time. "I suppose if I had messed up onstage that would have been entertaining, too," he says. "I've messed up a little where I've bled, but I've never had to go to the hospital."

HOW THE DAREDEVIL DOES IT

These instructions are for reading entertainment only. They are not to be followed, nor do they convey the full extent of knowledge and training required to attempt these dangerous acts.

Checklist: one 14-to-16-gauge nonporous steel surgical skewer that measures six to eight inches long, sharpened at one end; bandages; disinfectant spray

1. Study a book on anatomy and find out where the arteries and nerve bundles are in your biceps. Better

yet, consult a physician or someone who is familiar with artery and nerve location.

2. Hold your arm out and relax. Do not flex the muscle.

3. Push the sharpened end of the skewer slowly through your skin near the top of your biceps, avoiding arteries and nerve bundles (see Fig. 6). Keep pushing until the skewer goes all the way through the muscle and out the other side of your arm. Show your audience.

4. Remove the skewer slowly.

5. If you start bleeding, apply the disinfectant spray and then bandage your arm.

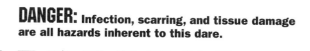

DANGER: Infection, scarring, and tissue damage are all hazards inherent to this dare.

Chapter 7

BODY BENDING IN A 13"x 16"x 19" BOX

With his unique talents, twenty-four-year-old Daniel Browning Smith has been capturing media attention for the past six years, with appearances on *Ripley's Believe It Or Not!, Guinness World Records Prime Time, The Tonight Show with Jay Leno, The Roseanne Show,* and even *Good Morning Singapore.* At five feet, eight inches tall and weighing 135 pounds, it would seem implausible that Smith could stuff himself into such a tiny box . . . implausible, but not impossible. "You have to be able to dislocate your arms and your legs," says Smith, "and you have to learn muscle control."

READ ALL ABOUT IT!

The inside of a sidewalk newspaper dispenser approximates the dimensions of a 13" x 16" x 19" box. Imagine dropping a coin into the slot, opening the latch for the morning paper, and finding a perfectly healthy human folded inside. This shockingly bizarre skill is expressly reserved for expert contortionists, people who can twist their bodies into extraordinary positions. Contortionists' anatomical anomalies have been astonishing spectators for millennia and remain a marvel in these modern times.

Smith has certainly earned his professional moniker, "The Rubberboy." In addition to his little-box stunt, Smith can get into a tied and chained straitjacket, and he can squeeze himself through a stringless tennis racket, or a toilet seat if you prefer. "Most [contortionists] train in only one direction," Smith says. "I'm an odd contortionist in that I can go in all directions. I can go forwards and backwards, and I can turn my head around back-

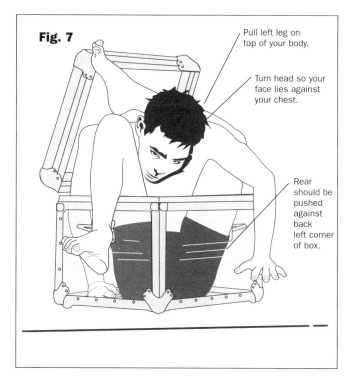

Fig. 7

Pull left leg on top of your body.

Turn head so your face lies against your chest.

Rear should be pushed against back left corner of box.

wards. The only part of my body that I can't look at is the top of my head and the back of my neck. My connective tissue is different, and when I dislocate my shoulder, it does not cause pain."

In 1998, after seeing the Bindlestiff Family Cirkus perform, Smith sold his belongings and joined the circus. Smith briefly indulged plans to study astrophysics, but the contortion bug grabbed hold of him early on. He was just four years old when his father watched him jump from the top of a bunk bed and do splits; the dad subsequently showed the son an old book with pictures of contortionists, which deeply intrigued the young body bender.

Smith's interest developed as his physique did. "In junior high school," Smith recalls, "I put my leg behind my head one day and some kid saw me and he said, 'Can you do that trick again?' I said, 'No,' and he said, 'I'll give you a piece of gum,' and I said, 'Wow, people will

give me gum and money for this.' It was intriguing to be able to do things that other people can't do. It was a fun way for me to meet girls and get everything for free."
Now, to earn his living, Smith sticks to a daily training routine to enhance his flexibility and to keep his body limber. "I have a natural flexibility, and on top of that, I train. I learned to tie my hands behind my back and tie them to a tree, and then walk backwards—a half inch at a time—until all my muscles and everything were stretched and my arms were completely over my head."

As with any job, there are occupational hazards, and one particular risk speaks to the extreme limits to which the daredevil contortionist goes: "When I get into the small-est box that I can get into," he says, "at one point I have to dislocate my right shoulder. Then there is so much pressure that I bleed through my skin."

BODY BENDING IN A 13"x 16"x 19" BOX

HOW THE DAREDEVIL DOES IT

These instructions are for reading entertainment only. They are not to be followed, nor do they convey the full extent of knowledge and training required to attempt these dangerous acts.

Checklist: box that measures 13" x 16" x 19"
(a transparent box is best for a live performance); ready assistant

1. Stand with both feet in the box, with your right hand on the right upper corner and your left hand on the left upper corner.

2. Squat down and put your hips in the left corner.

3. Raise your bent legs so you are sitting on your rear.

4. Push your rear against the back left corner and angle your body towards the front right corner.

5. Turn your head to the left and twist it so that your face is lying against your chest.

6. Lying on your right hand, which is twisted behind you, pull your left leg on top of your body.

(see Fig. 7). At this point, you might have to dislocate your right shoulder by pressing it against the side of the box. Pull your right leg inside the box and fold it underneath you.

7. Use your left hand to shut the door of the box, leaving your left arm and left leg folded over you like blankets.

DANGER: Muscle strains, burst blood vessels, and the wear and tear on skeletal joints and sockets are all risks of the extreme contortionist.

Chapter 8

BREAKING SIX 2-INCH-THICK CONCRETE SLABS AT ONCE WITH A HEAD BUTT

An ordained minister for a nondenominational church, forty-four-year-old Mike Hagen heads the Montana-based Mike Hagen Strength Team, a group of Christian bodybuilders who spread the word of Jesus by performing strongman feats, brick by brick, witness by witness. Team members bench-press while on beds of nails; they snap Louisville Slugger baseball bats in half with their hands; they rip apart giant phone books in seconds (see page 59). "This show won't change your life, but the message could," Hagen tells the crowd at the beginning of a typical two-hour act.

GARDEN-VARIETY PAIN

What better use is there for a nice clean slab of cement than to edge your garden? Why, to break it in half with your forehead, naturally! While it is a relatively simple stunt, breaking a stack of six two-inch-thick concrete edging slabs with one blow of the forehead is guaranteed to impress the neighbor.

In 1994, Hagen broke his arm in New Zealand while trying to karate-chop a stack of concrete blocks. It took him seven months of rehab to get the arm back into shape—a small cover charge to pay, perhaps, for eternal membership at Club Heaven.

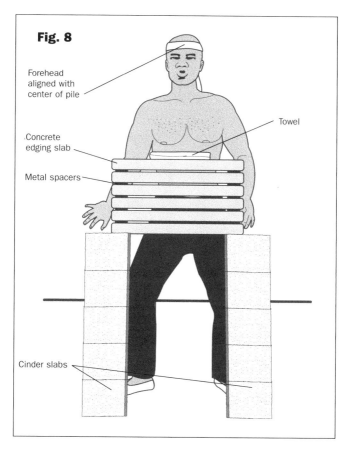

Fig. 8

Forehead aligned with center of pile

Towel

Concrete edging slab

Metal spacers

Cinder slabs

Another of Hagen's specialties is breaking concrete slabs with his forehead. The slabs, which are available at any home improvement store, are stacked six-high and are spaced with half-inch-square metal spacing bars. There must be slight spaces between the slabs; just stacking them on top of one another would create a wall of concrete that would be impossible to break. "If you just lay the slabs on top of each other, you wouldn't be able to break them with a sledgehammer," Hagen says.

The rest of it is all about focus and execution. Hagen concentrates on the pile of concrete slabs, knowing he must hit it with the hardest part of his head using a great amount of velocity. As with breaking bricks by a karate chop, he must swing from the hips.

HOW THE DAREDEVIL DOES IT

Checklist: ten or twelve cinder slabs; six 24″ x 8″ x 2″ concrete garden or edging slabs; towel

1. Stack two rows of cinder slabs as supports about waist high with twenty-one to twenty-two inches between the two stacks.

2. Put a two-inch-thick edging slab flat across the tops of the two rows of cinder blocks.

3. Place metal spacer bars at each end of the edging slab before adding a new block, and stack the remaining five blocks, with metal spacers between each one.

4. Place a towel on top of the stack of slabs and fold it over once.

5. Concentrate. Envision breaking the first slab you placed, the lowest in your pile.

6. Align your stance so that when you bend to the slabs, the middle of your forehead at the base of your hairline will hit the center of the towel-covered pile (see Fig. 8).

7. While thrusting your hips up and outward to leverage the force of your contact, slam your head down with great velocity.

8. Enjoy the sight of crumbled cement and take a bow.

DANGER: The head contains a very sensitive and essential organ known as the brain. When the head is subjected to multiple forceful impacts, the brain may suffer. Boxers, for example, are often known to suffer from brain damage later in life.

Chapter 9

LIFTING A 16-POUND BOWLING BALL BY THE EARLOBES

As one of five performing members of the Indianapolis-based Blue Monkey Sideshow, thirty-three-year-old Alan Rice—aka Mojo—stages a variety of nontraditional strongman feats. He swings bar stools attached to hooks pierced in his nipples; he pulls wheelchairs—with people in them—by rings in his ears; he even lifts bowling balls by chains attached to the tender-but-tough flesh of his earlobes.

LEND ME YOUR EAR

Some weight-lifting feats are less about the number of pounds than they are about the way the weight is hefted. This is especially true of flesh-suspension weight lifting: suspending weight via body piercings. There are many places in the human anatomy that can be pierced and used for the strange amusement of suspending heavy objects. The earlobe, for example, seems to serve no practical purpose but to offer a little real estate to showcase jewelry and other adornments. For some daredevils, the earlobe represents a tangible symbol of human possibilities—and how far those possibilities can be stretched.

"What I like about this stunt is not just that it defies pain," says Mojo, "but that it's also about training. Some people can accept the fact that athletes take years to train for running races in the Olympics; for me, this is very similar in that it shows how amazing the human body can be when it is properly trained."

Mojo says his anatomical fascination began in high school. "Ever since anthropology class, I've been messing with my body." Now dubbed Mojo the Human Freak or the Amazing Mojo, he shares his enthusiasm for the possibilities of the human body by demonstrating the capabilities of his own.

One of his most popular feats is earlobe lifting; among the objects he can lift by ear is a sixteen-pound bowling ball, along with the heavy chain used to attach the ball to his earlobes. "I have D-clips, or carabiner clips, attached to my ears." (D-clips are more commonly used for rock climbing and mountaineering purposes.) "Screwed into the bowling ball is an eyebolt. I use a six-foot-long metal chain, similar to logger chains, folded in half, to connect the bowling ball to the clips in my ears. It's not exactly comfortable."

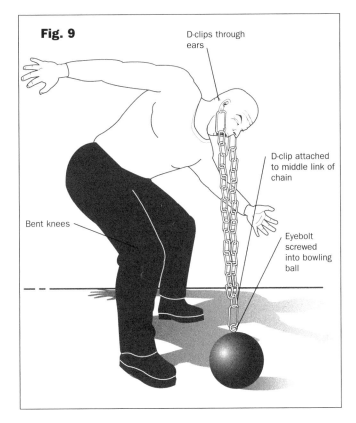

Fig. 9

D-clips through ears

D-clip attached to middle link of chain

Bent knees

Eyebolt screwed into bowling ball

For Mojo, lifting the ball is about focus and discipline. Fortunately, he hasn't torn apart his earlobes: "I think you get hurt when you try doing too much too fast, when you push yourself too hard. I've been lucky," he says. "I've been really lucky." Of course, luck is only part of the feat.

As with his nipple lifting, Mojo adheres to a general rule of thumb for flesh suspension: use an eight-to-ten-gauge hook for every ten pounds of weight. Like his training, the rest is a very gradual process. Mojo began his lobe lifting with a few pounds for each ear, and over the course of a few months, he continued to increase the weight. The stunt itself relies on the same spirit of gradation: "You have to lift it slowly and steadily," Mojo says. "You need to give the skin a chance to stretch along with the weight it is hoisting. Keep it moving, slow and steady. You must go slow and, at all costs, don't ever jerk the weight."

HOW THE DAREDEVIL DOES IT

These instructions are for reading entertainment only. They are not to be followed, nor do they convey the full extent of knowledge and training required to attempt these dangerous acts.

Checklist: sixteen-pound bowling ball; six-foot-long utility chain; eyebolt; three D-clips; two nimble earlobes

1. Pierce your ear and gradually increase the gauge of the piercing to open the hole wider.

2. When the holes are big enough, slip D-clips through your ears with the lever portions facing out.

3. Practice lifting various objects of gradually increasing weight.

4. When you feel that your lobes are ready for the bowling ball (this could take months), prepare the bowling ball by screwing an eyebolt into its surface.

5. Attach a D-clip to the eyebolt.

6. Fold a six-foot-long utility chain in half and attach it

at its center link to the D-clip on the bowling
ball.

7. With the ball on the floor, bend your knees and
    attach the other ends of the chain to the D-clips in
    your ears (see Fig. 9).

8. Proceed very slowly and steadily to lift the ball,
    avoiding any sudden jerking movement, giving your
    audience time to marvel at your ability.

DANGER: There is danger in tearing through the
flesh of the earlobe; subsequent to that danger is
the danger of dropping a sixteen-pound bowling
ball onto your foot; subsequent to that danger is
the danger of falling over in a sudden reaction to
the pain in your foot and injuring your head or
other body parts.

LIFTING A 16-POUND BOWLING BALL BY THE EARLOBES

Chapter 10

BLOWING FIRE

At age eighteen, Ted Shred joined a circus, and in the two decades that followed, he enjoyed a wide range of job experiences running the gamut from circus sideshow performer to rock band manager. Today, the forty-one-year-old is a circus owner and a professional daredevil whose skills have landed him appearances in Hollywood blockbusters such as *The Scorpion King* and both *Charlie's Angels* movies.

KISS OF FIRE

Fire-blowing is as dangerous to perform as it is impressive to watch. Combine a human element with toxic chemicals and fire and you have a popular recipe for danger: a human fountain spouting flame. The spectacle calls to daredevils the world over and is a mainstay of the sideshow circuit.

While he has learned much on his own through his adventurous life, Shred owes his initial interest in fire breathing to Gene Simmons. He was fourteen, and front and center at a Kiss concert—a dream come true for any American teenager in 1977. At the show's end, Shred was amazed when Simmons, the lead singer, blew fire out of his mouth. Then he smelled something: "It smelled like kerosene or

lighter fluid. I said, 'This is cool. I wonder if I can do it.'" He went home, practiced the stunt, and found out that, indeed, he could do it, and he's been doing it ever since.

Shred takes his fire-blowing seriously and is protective of the recipe for his secret fuel concoction. "People will use Coleman fuel or lighter fluid or Everclear alcohol. In

Mexico, they will even use gasoline," he says. "I use a secret mixture of oil and fuel. These mixtures are toxic, and can affect the liver and kidneys, so I have my blood tested twice a year to make sure my liver is okay. I can get away with using half a shot glassful of fuel. I can get four to six eight-foot-long blasts with that." His torch is a good old-fashioned rag on a stick soaked in a combination of Coleman fuel and oil.

To perform his fire-breathing feat, Shred takes a bit of the fuel concoction in his mouth and sprays a fine mist across the top of the flaming torch. He can blow all the fuel out of his mouth at once to create a large stream of fire, or he can puff in short bursts to create several consecutive fire streams. His longest fire shot is an amazing twenty-eight feet.

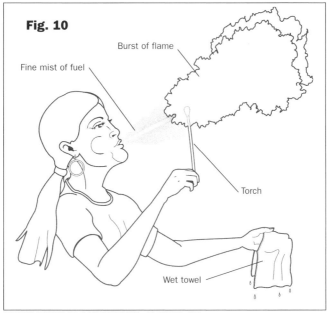

Fig. 10

Burst of flame

Fine mist of fuel

Torch

Wet towel

HOW THE DAREDEVIL DOES IT

These instructions are for reading entertainment only. They are not to be followed, nor do they convey the full extent of knowledge and training required to attempt these dangerous acts.

Checklist: fuel; shot glass; torch; wet towel; antiseptic rinse

1. Climate and clothing should be conducive to fire-breathing. Do it on a dry, windless day of about sixty to seventy degrees and wear cotton or fire-retardant clothing. (Do not wear nylon or spandex, which can melt onto your skin if it catches on fire.)

2. Prepare materials: a shot glass half filled with grain alcohol or other fuel mixture, a lighted torch, and a wet towel placed over one arm (in case you catch on fire).

3. Put the fuel in your mouth, but do not swallow.

4. Tip your head backward at a forty-five- to fifty-degree angle.

5. Hold the torch about three to six inches away from your mouth.

6. Purse your lips as tightly as possible. Then blow the fuel out of your mouth in as fine a mist as possible over the top of the torch. The fuel will catch fire when it comes into contact with the flame on your torch (see Fig. 10). The streaming spectacle of fire should last about three or four seconds.

7. Spit out any remaining fuel left in your mouth. Be sure not to swallow any of it.

8. Rinse mouth thoroughly, first with water, then with antiseptic.

DANGER: In addition to the evident external burn hazards of playing with fire, this stunt brings with it an array of less obvious threats: Your mouth can absorb the toxins in the fuel and cause long-term internal organ damage, and one inadvertent inhalation of the flame can char your lungs worse than a lifelong cigarette habit. You risk not only burning your mouth, but also collapsing a lung and the subsequent shock that can cause a fatal heart attack.

Chapter 11

WALKING ON HOT COALS

A leading authority on walking over hot coals, fifty-six-year-old Tolly Burkan heads the not-for-profit organization F.I.R.E., the Firewalking Institute of Research and Education. Burkan, who has appeared on many television talk shows and even taught the stunt to self-help guru Tony Robbins, uses firewalking as a metaphor for overcoming fears. Following a profound depression and two suicide attempts, Burkan began fighting fear with fire in 1977. That year, an article on firewalking in *Scientific American* piqued his interest, and a subsequent trip to India and the Far East turned that curiosity into a passion. He now makes his living teaching corporate seminars on firewalking and is considered the world's foremost trainer of firewalking instructors.

SOLES, COALS, AND RIGMAROLES

The seemingly primitive activity of walking over hot coals dates as far back as ancient India, and the fiery feat now attracts scores of modern-day followers. Those who practice the ritual are not always motivated by the same factors that inspire so many other daredevils. Instead, some firewalkers argue that what they do is a practice in self-empowerment and life affirmation.

"At first, I assumed it was a magic trick," Burkan says. "But as I researched it more, I realized it was not a trick." He came to believe that firewalking is the ultimate exercise in putting mind over matter. "Firewalking demonstrates how your thoughts impact everything else in your life," Burkan reports on his Web site. "Thoughts change brain chemistry, and that results in an alteration of body chemistry as well. Positive thinkers literally live in a different chemical environment than negative thinkers."

However, positive thinking doesn't necessarily equal fireproof feet: the stunt is not achieved through psychic fortitude alone. Scientific theory holds that the burning-hot coals used in the ritual do not have a high enough heat conductivity concentration—as opposed to, say, a metal barbecue grill—to intensely penetrate the insulation of the soles of human feet, especially when those soles aren't lingering in one place too long. Like the coals, human flesh is not a great conductor of heat.

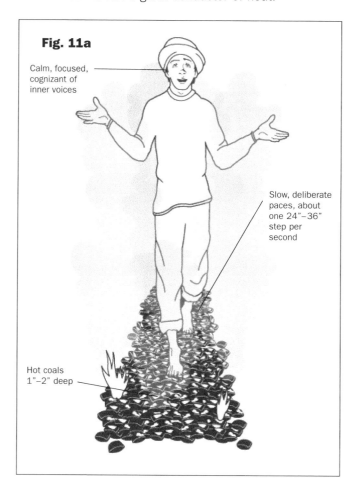

Fig. 11a

Calm, focused, cognizant of inner voices

Slow, deliberate paces, about one 24"–36" step per second

Hot coals 1"–2" deep

Physiology aside, Burkan maintains that one's mental state is key. If you are not mentally prepared, he cautions—if you feel like you cannot do it—then don't even try it. "When people are not in the state of mind that allows all body systems to operate at peak performance, the capillaries constrict and prevent the blood from moving freely through the tissue on the soles of the feet," he explains. "When that occurs, the blood cannot carry heat away from the sole and cannot maintain the temperature required to prevent burning. The result can be blistering or charring of the skin."

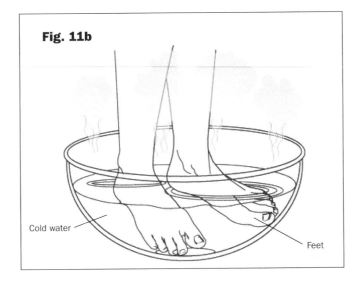

Fig. 11b

Cold water

Feet

HOW THE DAREDEVIL DOES IT

These instructions are for reading entertainment only. They are not to be followed, nor do they convey the full extent of knowledge and training required to attempt these dangerous acts.

Checklist: hot coals; mental clarity and vigor; dry feet; a tub or bucket of cold water; and, in case of injury, aloe vera, which contains properties that can restore circulation and, when applied immediately after a burn is sustained, prevent painful blistering

1. Prepare an eight- to ten-foot-long bed in which to burn a quarter cord of chopped cedar for sixty to ninety minutes, or until all the wood is burnt and only glowing coals remain.

2. Rake the coals evenly to a depth of between one and two inches within the bed.

3. Remove your socks and shoes; roll up your pant legs; try to relax and take some deep breaths.

4. Listen to your inner voices, and pay attention to the state of your body.

5. If you are not feeling calm and confident, do not proceed. Try to calm your mind.

6. Once you are confident and at peace with your decision to walk, proceed to walk over the coals, neither too fast nor too slow (see Fig. 11a). (Walking too fast may bury your feet in the coals, too slowly may burn them.)

7. After the walk, immerse your feet in cold water (see Fig. 11b).

DANGER: Charring and blistering of the feet are not only painful in their own right, these injuries, if severe, can seriously impair pedestrian mobility.

II.

STRENGTH, DEXTERITY, AND BALANCE

Chapter 12

ESCAPING PLASTIC WRAP MUMMIFICATION

A veteran of sideshow performances, fifty-three-year-old Harley Newman has mastered dozens of circus stunts. He shaves his face with fire; he walks barefoot over the sharp blades of swords; he can hold his weight upon the least number of nails—one! He is one of those rare beings whose extraordinary talents perfectly complement his distinctive fearless lunacy, and he puts on a show that audience members are not likely to forget. Fifteen years ago, Newman came up with the concept of escaping from plastic wrap.

TRANSPARENT ESCAPE

Escape art is as broad as the world of art itself, and encompasses a wide range of genres, styles, and media. There are traditional handcuff and straitjacket escapes; there are less traditional escapes that build on old-school styles, such as the handcuff escape inside a running laundry machine (see page 63). Then there are entirely original escapes, such as one from inside a tightly wound cocoon of plastic wrap.

"I saw these giant plastic bags and was reminded of an old escape act that Houdini did with a giant paper bag. I thought it would be a much more impressive act to allow the audience to see me, or at least my wrapped-up body, than to be completely out of sight where trickery could take place. I thought, 'Plastic wrap. . .' and then I thought, 'Yes, plastic wrap!'"

To perform the stunt, Newman sits barefoot or wearing only socks (no shoes), cross-legged, with his arms fold-

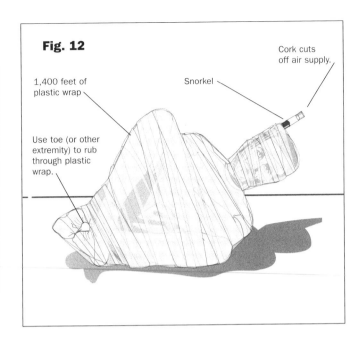

Fig. 12

Cork cuts off air supply.

1,400 feet of plastic wrap

Snorkel

Use toe (or other extremity) to rub through plastic wrap.

ed and his hands near his shoulders. Then he instructs seven audience participants, each with a two-hundred-foot roll of plastic wrap, to begin wrapping him, starting from the bottom and moving up. As they get closer to his face, he has a snorkel inserted into his mouth. When he's all sealed up, a cork gets jammed into the snorkel and cuts off his air supply. "People panic," he says. "They think I'm going to die."

"There are so many different layers that become between an inch and an inch and a half thick," he says. "It's hot and sticky inside. Further into the routine, it becomes grueling. There's no air; no ability to move; it's like you're frozen in concrete and you can't do much of anything but sit there."

One key is Newman's ability to hold his breath for long periods of time. (He can hold his breath for five minutes comfortably, and his personal record is over seven minutes.) But before the snorkel is corked, he does a series of hyperventilation exercises, breathing deeply and quickly, to increase oxygen to his blood and decrease the carbon dioxide. This allows for a little more time holding his breath.

Newman tells his audience he'll get out within two and a half minutes, and audience members are encouraged to hold their breath too. After about four and a half minutes, he can sense the audience's fear. "People get panicky," he says. "A lot of times, people are so freaked out they rush the stage to help me."

And while Newman has only been in trouble three times out of some 1,700 performances, he admits that it is a very dangerous strain. "You will hurt your body. The question is not 'Will I hurt myself?' The questions are 'When and how badly will I hurt myself?'"

The trick to the escape is concentrating on where the cocoon is most vulnerable. Because it is so hot, Newman can sense where the slightest bit of cooler temperature is seeping in and that becomes his target. H will wiggle a toe, a finger, maybe an elbow, and slow laboriously, rub against his cocoon until the layers weakening, breaking apart one by one. The first audience will see of him is a finger poking thro wrap, or a foot, or a hand. "I finally rip the w off my body and then peel it off my head, w painful," he says. "My face is always crim soaked in sweat, but I am always extrem an audience, who seem extremely hap

HOW THE DAREDEVIL DOES IT

These instructions are for reading entertainment only.
convey the full extent of knowledge and training re

Checklist: seven two-hundre
seven volunteers to wrap y

1. Sit down cross-legge
    your chest.

2. Instruct the volu
    top, tilting you

3. Begin hyperventilating, breathing in deep, quick, measured breaths, to increase the oxygen in your blood.

4. Have a snorkel placed in your mouth before your head is wrapped.

5. When you're all wrapped up, have a cork placed in the snorkel, cutting off your air.

6. Stay calm and focus on the environment within the cocoon, then slowly begin rubbing a spot closest to where you feel the coolest area in the cocoon (see 12).

MIFICATION

 the spot until you are able to burst layers of the cocoon.

 by enlarging the initial

 the

begin
thing the
ugh the
ole thing
ich is very
son red and
ely happy to see
by to see me."

they are not to be followed, nor do they
quired to attempt these dangerous acts.

d-foot rolls of plastic wrap:
u; snorkel; cork
, with your arms folded ar

nteers to roll you up fror
as necessary to wrap yr

Chapter 13

RIPPING A PHONE BOOK IN HALF IN LESS THAN TEN SECONDS

Their message is one of love and it is proclaimed loudly in their massive, bulging biceps and their high-energy demonstrations of strength. Buff disciples, the Montana-based Mike Hagen Strength Team (see page 40) consists of twelve bodybuilders dedicated to winning over more believers for Jesus.

PAPER WASTREL

From Samson to Conan to Tarzan, great feats of strength and brute power have always impressed. While such vigorous displays normally involve serious unrestrained might, one remarkable strongman feat requires more method than muscle: ripping a gigantic phone book in half in a matter of seconds.

In packed auditoriums, members of the Strength Team smash concrete blocks to pieces with perfectly timed karate chops. They do bench presses while lying on beds of nails. Bare-handed, they bend steel rods and horseshoes, snap Crescent wrenches in half, roll up frying pans, break baseball bats, smash through walls of ice, and rip apart phone books. Their physical exhibitions are intended to rile and inspire their audience and to encourage the crowd to destroy their own spiritual obstacles and personal demons.

"We're going to defeat the Devil tonight!" a voice commands through a reverberating speaker system at a typical demonstration. "Give me a 'J!' Give me an 'E!' Give me an 'S!' Give me a 'U!' Give me an 'S!' What's that spell?"

"Jesus!" the audience shouts.

As head of the Strength Team, Mike Hagen is not your ordinary preacher. The forty-four-year-old former fullback for the NFL's Seattle Seahawks answered his unusual calling in 1984 when he joined the Power Team, a group of athletes and strongmen based in Dallas, Texas. Similar to the Strength Team, this group employs strongmen and former professional athletes to get people's attention and preach the Word.

The Mike Hagen Strength Team was formed in November 2000. The team visits hundreds of schools a year in an attempt to keep kids out of gangs and trouble. "We use strength as a tool to communicate with people who may not normally attend church," Hagen says.

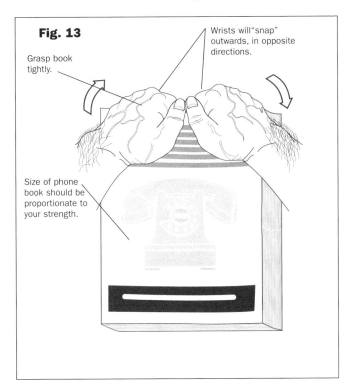

Fig. 13

Grasp book tightly.

Wrists will "snap" outwards, in opposite directions.

Size of phone book should be proportionate to your strength.

One of Hagen's signature stunts is ripping large phone books completely in half in remarkably short periods of time. He does this with astonishing ease, but infused with plenty of pumped-up pomp. During a show in Albuquerque, New Mexico, he ripped apart six 1,500-page phone books in forty-three seconds. This is a standard strongman stunt that is relatively easy to do: "You just hit it and pop it, rolling with your wrists," Hagen explains. "It's all in the technique."

HOW THE DAREDEVIL DOES IT

These instructions are for reading entertainment only. They are not to be followed, nor do they convey the full extent of knowledge and training required to attempt these dangerous acts.

Checklist: a telephone book compatible in size with your abilities

1. Start small—with the directory for a small town for example; gradually work yourself up to something the size of Manhattan's mammoth phone book.

2. Grasp the book tightly with both hands and hold it out in front of your body. The binding should be facing the left, and the book should be parallel to the floor.

3. Wrap your fingers around the book's front edge and onto its back, and rest your thumbs on the front. Hands should be close together, almost touching (see Fig. 13).

4. Make sure there is no slack in the pages—the book should be compressed as densely as possible.

5. Envision the technique: You will snap your wrists apart and roll them outwards in opposite directions. Snapping means pulling the book apart with a short, quick burst of energy, not a slow tear.

6. Do the snap quickly: initial velocity is everything in this stunt. If you've done it correctly, the top portion of the pages will rip down the book's middle. (Remember, you are not ripping the spine: the pages should split down the middle.)

7. Once you get the slight rip going, quickly and force-fully roll your wrists outward in opposite directions and proceed to rip the book down the middle.

8. Do as many series of quick wrist rolls as you can until the book is torn in half within ten seconds.

ON PRACTICING: Practice without a book in hand. Hold hands in front of yourself and pretend you are grasping the book. Then do a quick pull apart, or snap with your hands. Then just do a wrist roll; that is, roll your wrists outward in opposite directions.

DANGER: Immediate hazards include muscle strain and the potential wrath of the next person looking for the phone book; long-term dangers may include repetitive stress injuries.

Chapter 14

ESCAPE FROM A RUNNING WASHING MACHINE WHILE RESTRAINED IN HAND-CUFFS AND LEG IRONS

Forty-six-year-old Rick Maisel is a professional escape artist who set a world record in 1996 by freeing himself from a straitjacket while hanging upside down, suspended from a bar, in a hasty 2.23 seconds. Since the late 1980s, Maisel, of Albuquerque, New Mexico, has performed the laundry escape while restrained in seven pairs of handcuffs and two pairs of leg irons thousands of times in thirty-six countries. He even performed the stunt, wearing a suit and tie, on a TV commercial for laundry detergent.

A SQUEAKY-CLEAN GETAWAY

Good escape scenarios produce total suspense. Harry Houdini built his legendary career largely on his preternatural ability to escape from life-threatening situations: known as the handcuff king, he could extricate himself from sunken crates, padded cells, coffins, rolltop desks, burglarproof safes, iron boilers, diving suits, and U.S. mail pouches, to name a few. When it comes to escape feats, the more absurdly dangerous the scenario, the better, which makes the washing machine an ideal setting for suspense: if the daredevil does not escape before the machine goes into its spin cycle, he could die in a matter of seconds.

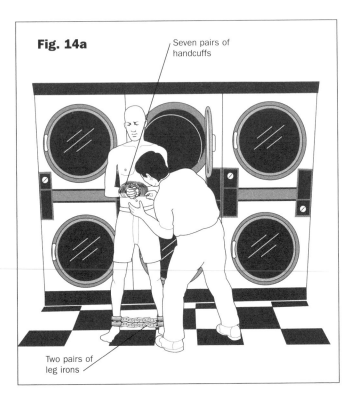

Fig. 14a

Seven pairs of handcuffs

Two pairs of leg irons

Maisel's parallel career as a locksmith helped provide the keys to his entrée into escape artistry. He has studied the patent designs on virtually every brand of handcuff and leg iron on the planet. He designs his own picking tools, but he swears he doesn't use them in his washing-machine stunt, nor does he use a key.

The artistry involved in escaping restraints and handcuffs remains a mystery to those who don't practice it. Maisel is not quick to lift the shroud of mystery, but he says that he understands the weaknesses in certain design patents, and this helps him tap locks open. Most locks contain pins and tumblers that, with practice, can be manipulated with a pick or tapped open by applying the right combination of torque and pressure. Either method requires practice and patience to learn, and Maisel strongly suggests expertise in lock-picking before attempting to escape handcuffs while in a washing machine.

Fig. 14b

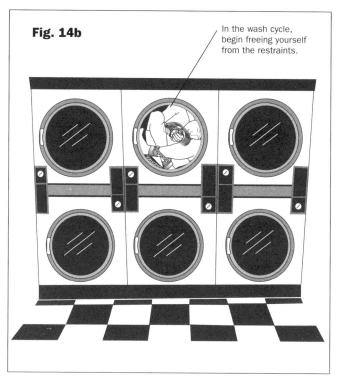

In the wash cycle, begin freeing yourself from the restraints.

Additionally, some cuffs are flawed by design and can be slipped through, even when they are on tightly. Maisel suggests that a beginner go to an army surplus store and buy a pair of cuffs (along with many sets of extra keys, since keys can break) and practice various methods of escaping.

Maisel trained for about a year before actually performing the washing-machine escape. First he had to overcome motion sickness: When he first started developing the stunt, he could only spend about sixty seconds in the machine. He gradually conditioned himself to endure thirty-two minutes inside the wet, rotating belly of the beast.

"I see everything in slow motion," he says. "I have to escape before the machine goes into the spin cycle, which will kill me in three to five seconds. Most machines go at 450 rpm's in the spin cycle, and that represents seventy-two G forces."

Maisel has never been injured performing the stunt, but he did have one close call on the set of a TV show in the late 1990s. "The on/off switch broke off the machine and I had to get out before the spin cycle kicked in. They were able to turn the machine off at the power source."

When asked what he has learned from his experiences, Maisel says: "I've come up with a design for what I think is a better washing machine. Oh, and DON'T TRY THIS AT HOME!"

HOW THE DAREDEVIL DOES IT

These instructions are for reading entertainment only. They are not to be followed, nor do they convey the full extent of knowledge and training required to attempt these dangerous acts.

Checklist: front-loading, commercial washing machine with a twelve-inch door and a twenty-four-inch drum; seven pairs of handcuffs; two pairs of leg irons; trusty assistant; intimate knowledge of lock technology

1. Fill the washing machine three-quarters full with warm, soapy water. Most machines hold between eight to ten gallons of water.

2. Have your assistant lock seven pairs of handcuffs on you.

3. Have your assistant lock two pairs of leg irons on you (see Fig. 14a).

DEAD END
BRAIN ZONE

4. With help from your assistant, stuff yourself into the machine and close the door.

5. Have your assistant add the final two gallons of water into the top of the machine.

6. Have assistant turn on the wash cycle.

7. Focus on one lock at a time: by picking, tapping, or slipping out, free yourself from the two sets of cuffs closest to the wrist (see Fig. 14b).

8. Subsequent cuffs should be easier to slip out of since they have been locked into place on gradually larger circumferences of the lower forearm. Remove each.

9. Focus on picking, tapping, or slipping out of the leg irons, one pair at a time.

10. Give a signal through glass door to alert your assistant that you are free.

11. When the assistant opens the door, dive out of the machine, leaving the cuffs and leg irons behind.

12. Resist thoughts of getting into the dryer.

DANGER: Confining yourself in a small space where soapy water is constantly around you can lead to the inadvertent swallowing of chemicals and potentially drowning. Also, the shifting drum inside the machine can cause injuries to the head, spine, and other vital areas of the body.

ESCAPE FROM A RUNNING WASHING MACHINE WHILE RESTRAINED IN HANDCUFFS AND LEG IRONS

Chapter 15

BALANCING 75 PINT GLASSES ON THE CHIN

Ashrita Furman manages a health food store in Jamaica, New York—which seems like a mere sidebar next to what he does when he isn't working. In his fifty years of life, Furman has held over eighty world records, including some of the wackiest ever documented: he joggled (jogging while simultaneously juggling) for 50 miles; he somersaulted the entire 12.2 miles of Paul Revere's revered route in Massachusetts; for 16 miles he pogo-sticked up and down the foothills of Mount Fuji; he invented a category for the *Guinness Book of World Records* when he pogo-sticked underwater in the Amazon River (see page 158); he once held the record for the most number of squats performed in one hour (3,038), which he happened to do while in a hot-air balloon; he sack-raced for 6.2 miles along the foot of Mount Rushmore; and in 1987, he was awarded a record for the most Guinness records in different categories. In fact, when he was interviewed for this book, he was preparing for a trip to Paris to break a record for the most abdominal crunches in one hour. Yet, with all of his zany tests of endurance, one of

LEANING TOWER OF PINTS
This stunt—or a lesser version of it—probably started as a small-time barroom shenanigan. But when it comes to balancing eighteen feet of leaning glass, this dare is a pretty tall order to fill.

the trickiest tests he takes is the balancing of pint glasses on his chin. He holds the world's record for stacking 75 twenty-ounce "pint" glasses this way.

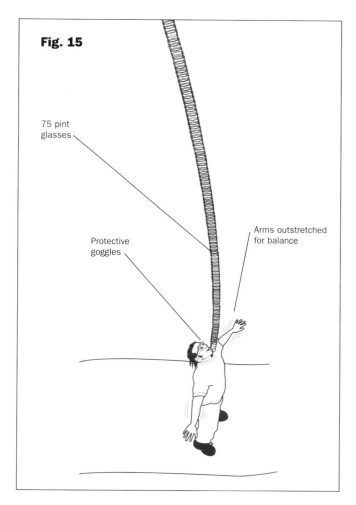

Fig. 15

75 pint glasses

Protective goggles

Arms outstretched for balance

"It's extremely difficult, and it's dangerous," Furman says. And it's unpredictable. "The glass is very tempera-ture-sensitive. If it's too hot or too cold, the structural properties of the glass are compromised. The glasses can crack and break much more easily." The ideal tem-perature, he says, is between fifty and sixty degrees Fahrenheit.

In addition to temperature, there is the consideration of the logistics for preparing the dare. Furman has built a special shelf attached to his house for the sole purpose of stacking pint glasses. The shelf is an L-shaped pair of long wood strips that rest at a very slight angle against the house and run vertically to above the roof. The shelf bottom is fixed at chin level. When performing the dare, he stacks the glasses on the shelf first; then he hoists them, as a unit, onto his chin. He has on hand a trusty assistant who is perched high on a ladder toward the top of the shelf; the helper is there to salvage falling glasses in case of an emergency. "The glasses are expensive," Furman says. "They cost more than a buck apiece!"

But it is not just a sense of thrift that drives Furman to avoid breaking his glasses. It is very dangerous to have a sixty-pound, fifteen-foot-high stack of glass precariously balanced directly above your head. "As glasses crack from high above you, you can easily get blinded or suffer a bad cut to your neck" from broken shards, he says. "And at seventy-five glasses, the pressure of the glass is really at its breaking point."

Furman is happy with the seventy-five glasses that he can balance—for the time being at least. Why does he feel so compelled to break records? Because the feats create a sense of spiritual challenge and adventure, for which he prepares through disciplined meditation. Furman is a longtime student of Sri Chinmoy, an Eastern-inspired guru whose teachings are about self-transcendence. "It's about going beyond what you believe are your limits," he says. "Ashrita"—the name he was given by his master—is a Sanskrit word that means "protected by God."

HOW THE DAREDEVIL DOES IT

These instructions are for reading entertainment only. They are not to be followed, nor do they convey the full extent of knowledge and training required to attempt these dangerous acts.

Checklist: high vertical shelf; seventy-five pint glasses; air temperature between fifty and sixty degrees Fahrenheit; goggles; ladder; trusty assistant to catch the glasses from the top end if the tower begins to fall

1. Build a long, vertical shelf on which to stack the glasses.

2. Stack the glasses, climbing the ladder as necessary. Have your assistant stand at the top of the ladder when the stack is complete.

3. Back on the ground, strap on some goggles.

4. At chin level, where the bottom of the shelf is aligned, grab the bottom glass firmly.

5. Place your other hand as high up as possible on the stack and get a grip around it.

6. Pull the stack off the shelf very gently, allowing the top to lean in the direction it chooses.

7. Carefully bring the tower to your face as you raise your chin to meet it.

8. Hold the tower on your chin until it assumes a steady position. Focus on the highest part of the tower visible to you.

9. Let go of the glass and balance the tower on your chin with as little movement as possible for ten seconds (see Fig. 15).

10. Grab the stack and carefully return it to the shelf.

DANGER: Heavy glass shards can easily lodge in your body and cut you if gravity brings the glasses crashing down.

Chapter 16

WALKING A TIGHTROPE, BLINDFOLDED, WITHOUT A NET

A traveling circus troupe consisting of acrobats, jugglers, and clowns, the Wallenda family traces its performance roots to the Austro-Hungarian Empire of the late 1700s. In the 1930s and '40s, the "Great Wallendas" were headliners with Ringling Bros. and Barnum & Bailey Circus. After one slippery incident during which four members fell on the wire, but were not seriously injured, a news article reported, "The Wallendas fell so gracefully that it seemed as if they were flying." Today, the "Flying Wallendas" are synonymous with the high wire.

BLIND, HIGH AND WIRED

An old favorite of the circus, tightrope—or high wire—walking finds its origins in ancient Egypt. It is a traditional stunt that has endured because it showcases a very pure and true talent that is, in its simplest form, about keeping one's balance under extreme conditions. It is a visceral metaphor for navigating life itself.

A multigenerational act, the Wallendas perform dazzling stunts at dizzying heights: they form human pyramids on a single wire; they ride bicycles across the wire while a relative stands balanced on the rider's shoulders; they walk the tightrope blindfolded.

To understand the "gravity" of walking the wire blind, one must first appreciate what is required to walk one with sight. "No wire walker ever looks down while performing;

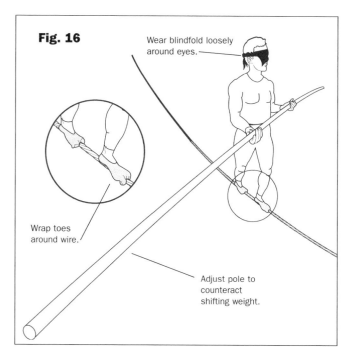

Fig. 16

Wear blindfold loosely around eyes.

Wrap toes around wire.

Adjust pole to counteract shifting weight.

it could spell disaster," says fifty-three-year-old Tino Wallenda. "You look ahead at a fixed point to help get your sense of balance."

Wallenda has walked on wires ranging from 250 to 1,200 feet in length. He does not use a net. To do this stunt, says Wallenda, "You have to be extremely focused—focused on the other side of the cable."

Keeping an eye on the fixed point, the walker, wearing moccasinlike footwear, positions his or her feet on the wire. The wire is very thin, and as one foot is placed in front of the other, most walkers curl their big toes around the wire. A metal balancing pole, which extends out to the sides of the walker's body, is often used. The pole, which can be as long as thirty feet and weigh as much as fifty pounds, is gripped tightly, with knuckles wrapped around the bottom. Some walkers hold the pole close to their bodies, a little over waist high; others hold it out farther from their bodies. The weight and length of the pole help the walker maintain equilibrium; as weight shifts to one side, the pole is shifted to the other side to offset the movement of the body.

But when walking without sight, watch out: "Walking blindfolded—truly blindfolded—is extremely difficult," says Wallenda. "There are three components to balance. There is your touch, your vision, and your inner ear. If you lose one of the three, you can still get to the other end, but you do it clumsily.

Instead, most tightrope walkers use a looser blindfold that allows a glimpse of something, if only a flash of light at the bottom of the blindfold. "Because you can usually see something, that aspect of it gives you your assurance and your balance," says Wallenda. You must rely more faithfully on the feel of the wire beneath your weight, and on the inner equilibrium that guides you to adjust your balancing pole as needed. Key advice: proceed with caution.

SANE PEOPLE
KEEP RIGHT
OF THIS

HOW THE DAREDEVIL DOES IT

These instructions are for reading entertainment only. They are not to be followed, nor do they convey the full extent of knowledge and training required to attempt these dangerous acts.

Checklist: aircraft cable five-eighths of an inch in diameter; fasteners for the cable (the cable should be attached to something sturdy, such as a brick wall or an iron pole pounded into the ground); balancing poles measuring from twenty to thirty feet long, weighing twenty to fifty pounds; moccasinlike footwear; blindfold; safety net; platform

1. Put on the moccasinlike footwear, and practice by walking normally over a wire raised only a few feet from the ground. Learn to get the feel of the wire under your feet, and practice wrapping your big toe around the wire.

2. As you become more experienced, practice with your eyes closed.

3. Set up a safety net, and start performing the stunt at progressively higher elevations.

4. When you feel confident that you can keep your balance for a full walk across the wire, set up the wire at an elevation of twenty-five feet and set up a platform at the same height. Climb up the ladder to the platform.

5. Put a blindfold over your eyes. It should be somewhat loose so you can still see something that will help you maintain your balance.

6. Grasp the balancing pole at its center with your knuckles gripped around the pole's bottom.

7. Slowly step off the platform and cautiously use your toes to feel the wire.

8, Proceed to step forward carefully, placing one foot in front of the other, wrapping your toes around the wire. Adjust the balancing pole as necessary; if you lean to the left, shift the balancing pole out to the right, and vice versa (see Fig. 16). Don't look straight down!

9. When you become an expert at walking across the wire at twenty-five feet, try the stunt without the net.

DANGER: Falling from heights is a common fear; for the net-free, high-wire walker, it is an occupational hazard that has exacted a wicked toll on many in the form of death, broken bones, and paralysis.

Chapter 17

JUGGLING CHAINSAWS

Daredevil extraordinaire and world-class juggler Dick Franco has been performing the stunt for over two decades. "To answer your questions," he pronounces on his Web site, "YES. . . they are real! YES . . . the blades are sharp! YES . . . they will cut me! YES . . . I have been cut!"

"SPLIT"-SECOND REFLEXES

Chainsaw juggling may sound like a terrible oxymoron, a contradiction in terms, like "nice mother-in-law" or "Michael Jackson's natural features and pedestrian lifestyle." But for a few select daredevils, the two words go hand in cautious hand. There are methods to the madness, and they begin only after a complete mastery of juggling techniques has been achieved. Unlike your average circus juggler, the chainsaw juggler requires more than just balls.

Franco may rightly be credited with inventing (perhaps not "single-handedly") the stunt of chainsaw juggling. Working the entertainment circuit in Reno, Nevada, in 1983, Franco got the idea while walking past a lawn mower store where a gas-powered chainsaw beckoned to him. "It was very heavy . . . about twelve pounds, but it felt good in the hand and had a big handle that I thought I could catch. I bought it and took it home to see what I could do with it." After making some adjustments to the machine, Franco brought it to the hotel where he worked to practice tossing it. "When the cast and showroom staff saw me practice, the hotel was 'buzzing' about it! I was determined to find a way to juggle three of them," Franco says.

But it was more than just a matter of juggling three dangerous, awkwardly balanced, oddly shaped items.

"The saw was very heavy at one end with the center [of gravity] where the engine flywheel turned," says Franco. "This left the blade end protruding a good ten inches off balance, which put the sharp teeth that much closer to me. I decided to fashion an additional handle that would put the tip of the blade [farther] away from my hand when thrown in a single revolution and caught."

Even with the adjustments, Franco still had to contend with the weight of the saws. He'd juggled heavy objects like bowling balls in the past and knew that gradual strength conditioning was instrumental to success. He began upper-body weight training.

"I eventually gained the strength and timing to juggle two non-running saws and felt I was ready to try three. Because of the weight it was impossible to start in the conventional way by holding two saws in one hand. That would be twenty-four pounds in one hand! I decided to balance one saw on my chin and let it drop into the pattern as I threw the other two saws. On the first try the blade gave me a deep gash on the top of my forearm."

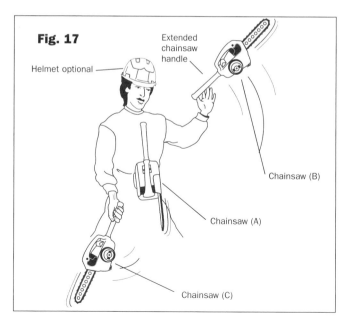

Fig. 17

Extended chainsaw handle

Helmet optional

Chainsaw (B)

Chainsaw (A)

Chainsaw (C)

But practice makes perfect. Franco constructed three wooden "chainsaws" with the same dimensions and features of the real ones and set to work. He soon realized that leg strength was as important as upper-body strength for catching and dipping with each throw. Gradually, he substituted three non-running chainsaws into his practice regime. Eventually, after resolving problems of maintaining steady idle speeds on the chainsaw motors, he began practicing cautiously with running chainsaws.

"The first time I juggled three running chainsaws, I was elated!" he recalls. "I discovered that I could juggle them much easier than ones that were not running. The rotation of the flywheel inside the engine and the rotation of the heavy chain blade created a gyroscopic stabilizing effect. . . . This made the path that each saw traveled when thrown much more predictable, with none of the side-to-side or twisting variations that I experienced while practicing with three saws that were not running. Once I got the hang of it, I even dented the clutch housings so they made permanent contact with the clutch. That meant that the blades would not stop . . . no matter what they came in contact with!"

Before he substituted battery-powered saws, his earlier gas-powered chainsaws set off a few sensitive smoke alarms. He has experienced some problems with tendonitis, some trouble in his elbows and lower back, and some near disasters on a few occasions. But in the two decades since he established his signature stunt, Franco has only dropped saws three times during regular performances.

HOW THE DAREDEVIL DOES IT

These instructions are for reading entertainment only. They are not to be followed, nor do they convey the full extent of knowledge and training required to attempt these dangerous acts.

Checklist: expert juggling skills; three battery-powered chainsaws of equal weight, with motors that can run at fixed speeds and custom-made, extending handles

1. Balance the extended handle of one chainsaw on your chin while holding the others in each hand.

2. Swing the right arm back to set the first throw.

3. At the same moment the right arm swings forward to release its saw (chainsaw C), let the chin-balanced chainsaw (chainsaw A) fall toward the right hand and catch it.

4. Toss the left-hand chainsaw up (chainsaw B) and use the left hand to catch the first tossed chainsaw, then juggle all three (see Fig. 17).

5. Count out eleven throws, the recommended sequence.

6. Prior to the last right-handed throw, hold onto the last saw to land in the left hand rather than preparing to toss it again.

7. Heave the last right-hand throw a bit higher and with a slower revolution.

8. Meanwhile, quickly catch the preceding fall with the right hand and hand it off to the left hand. (The handles of two saws in one hand will be heavy and awkward to hold.)

9. Catch the last saw in the right hand and take a bow.

DANGER: Chainsaws are heavy-duty tools used to cut through hard wood. The damage they can inflict on the human body is fodder for the horror-movie genre. Less obvious are the muscular strains and injuries that handling heavy chainsaws can cause.

Chapter 18

BALANCING A RUNNING LAWN MOWER ON THE FACE

As director and superstar of Circus Orange, a traveling collective of talented performers, technicians, and actors devoted to "spectacle" entertainment, Tom Comet balances extraordinary talent against dangerous and often pyrotechnic showmanship. In addition to juggling running chainsaws and blowtorches, he makes what has been called the world's most dangerous salad by balancing a running lawn mower on his face while audience members toss lettuce heads at the revolving blades.

BALANCED BLADES

From juggling to stilt walking to riding unicycles, a good sense of balance comes in handy under the big top, and wildly bizarre balancing acts are a staple of the circus industry. A good daredevil's balancing act must use an object that not only is challenging to balance but poses grave danger to the one who undertakes the challenge. A running lawn mower, balanced a mere handle's distance from the head, fits the bill.

"The trick to the lawn mower," says Comet, "is getting over the logistics and the fear, and getting over the fact that it is a loud, stinky, gas-powered machine. It is just another object that is longer than it is wide and therefore possible to balance on one's chin."

Obviously, practice in balancing objects on your chin or nose helps. Comet recommends starting simply with something lightweight that can be comfortably placed on your chin, on end, without causing pain. The key is that the object be longer than it is wide. Comet suggests using things such as long wooden dowels, lightweight brooms, and toilet plungers, preferably clean ones. "Another great choice is the peacock feather," Comet says, "because it is lightweight and there is the added bonus of wind resistance from the feathers, which make it fall slower and enables your reactions to be slower as well, which makes it easiest of all to learn."

Comet's optimistic outlook has undoubtedly helped him achieve success. While learning to balance any object, he says, "you will drop the object many, many times. The trick here is not to see this as a failure but rather one less time that you will have to bend down and pick that thing up before you overcome the physics involved and

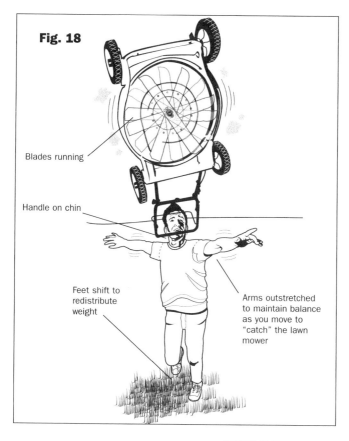

Fig. 18

Blades running

Handle on chin

Feet shift to redistribute weight

Arms outstretched to maintain balance as you move to "catch" the lawn mower

achieve the balance. Each 'failure' is in fact more experi-ence, and the more experience [you have], the closer you are to eventual success."

But in balancing lawn mowers, practice and repetition would not remedy the technical hurdles Comet encoun-tered. "You have to make the lawn mower run upside down, which is not something a lawn mower is meant to do. There is no upside-down grass, so why would the mower need to run this way outside of Tom Comet's lunatic stunt world?"

Comet had the gas tank and carburetor in his lawn mower customized to operate upside down, and put padding on the portion of the handle that rests on his chin. Still, motorized machines pose other inherent problems to maintaining equilibrium. "Lawn mowers vibrate like crazy," he says, "and when placed on the chin have a disconcert-ing ability to completely disorient you, causing your brain to actually forget that you are standing below an extremely dangerous machine. This is not good!"

After a few close calls, Comet has learned to stock spare parts, including gas caps, and to tighten and secure all bolts before each performance. As a result, there are perhaps few professional groundskeepers who take as good care of their lawn mowers as does Tom Comet.

HOW THE DAREDEVIL DOES IT

These instructions are for reading entertainment only. They are not to be followed, nor do they convey the full extent of knowledge and training required to attempt these dangerous acts.

Checklist: a securely bolted push lawn mower rigged to run upside down

1. While looking straight up, imagine the lawn mower balanced on your chin while your lower body moves around as fluidly as possible to keep it balanced.

2. Start your lawn mower engine.

3. Without letting go, bend your knees so that your chin is almost touching the handle, grab the sides of the handle, and slowly hoist the machine above you.

4. Hold the mower so that it is balanced on your chin. Focus on the top of the mower, and make sure that it is perfectly aligned with your body.

5. Let go.

6. As the mower begins leaning in one direction or another by the force of gravity, move in that direction to counteract the fall (see Fig. 18).

7. Slightly overcompensate to "catch" the object and straighten it again.

8. Continue this balancing act for as long as you are able to hold the lawn mower on your chin.

DANGER: The sharp blades of a lawn mower can instantaneously cut through flesh, cartilage, and even bone. One slip and the lawn mower can come crashing down with gore-inducing consequences. A hazard that is less apparent than the spinning blades is, in fact, the weight of the lawn mower itself. The precariously balanced, top-heavy weight is absorbed through neck muscles and sensitive tissue at the top of the spine, an area that is vulnerable to painful injury and long-term damage.

III.

TAMING THE WILD BEAST

Chapter 19

GROWING A BEARD OF BEES

G rowing beards is usually a man's specialty, but forty-four-year-old Jackie Park-Burris knows precisely how to mimic the chin whiskers her father used to make. "I started with my dad. We knew bees and we got a barber's apron and put it around his neck and hung a queen near his throat and dumped four pounds of bees on the apron."

EASY AS A, BEE!, C

If you're trying to grow a unique beard, this might be the stunt for you—the beloved, bloodcurdling bee beard. Smear a little queen bee pheromone on your face, let loose the bees, and voilà, your face is abuzz with beard.

That was twenty-three years ago, at the first annual Palo Cedro Honey Bee Festival in northern California. "My dad did it, and then my sister did it, and I helped them," says Park-Burris. "I have been doing this from Day One. I was always the person pouring the bees on the person doing it."

A third-generation member of a line of local beekeepers that dates back to the early 1900s, Park-Burris was next in line for the bee beard; bees were in her blood, so to speak. But doing it is more than just spectacle. The stunt is part of her way of educating people about bees and demonstrating that the insects are not the vicious and aggressive monsters they are often thought to be (though she does use her own Park Italian bees—especially bred to be gentle—to do the stunt).

The lesson is a strange and sensational one to teach. "They feel like tons of little suction cups crawling all over your face," she says. "They will chew on you. I have had them chewing on me and I've shouted, 'Knock it off. I've got to finish this.' They get on a certain part of your face and they like it and they will lick and chew you. Your face is always red when you get done with a bee beard." Park-Burris says she has only suffered a few occasional stings.

And, as a beekeeper, she can tell you a lot about the nature of hive mentality and the importance of the queen. "Bees want to be where the queen is because they know that they must constantly be reproducing because bees only live about six weeks," she says. "They know the queen is the producer; she lays eggs, and so they desire to be near her."

HOW THE DAREDEVIL DOES IT

These instructions are for reading entertainment only. They are not to be followed, nor do they convey the full extent of knowledge and training required to attempt these dangerous acts.

Checklist: between ten thousand and forty thousand bees, including the queen; insect repellent; an enclosed or netted area or a tent; sugar water; an assistant ready with a container of burlap to burn; a credit card; a funnel; a bag, box, or hive

Fig. 19a

Spread remains of queen bee across face.

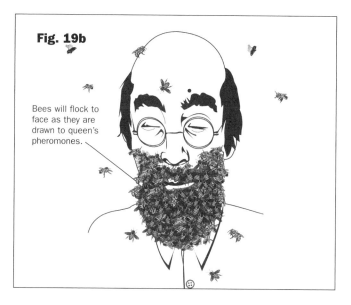

Fig. 19b

Bees will flock to face as they are drawn to queen's pheromones.

1. Obtain the queen bee from a hive. Queen bees are generally larger than the worker bees, and with more elongated bodies, so look for the largest bee in the hive. A good indicator is that she will be surrounded by drones.

2. After obtaining the queen bee, crush her and spread her remains on the part of your face where a beard would grow (see Fig. 19a). Avoid the eyes, ears, and nostrils.

3. Help shape the beard by applying insect repellent to the areas of your face where you do not want the bees.

4. Take the crushed queen corpse and put it near the base of your neck.

5. Put an apron around your neck, over the corpse.

6. Feed a hive of bees with sugar-water syrup beforehand, which will help calm them, then dump about four pounds of bees out of the hive onto the apron. (Hives can range from ten to twelve pounds.)

7. The bees will slowly climb onto your face in their instinct to be near the queen, whose pheromones have been spread across your face and whose scent still lingers from beneath the apron.

8. Bees can be scooped up with credit cards and moved from one spot to another; and they can be manipulated with smoke, which they do not like. Have your assistant use these methods to shape the beard.

DANGER
CRAZY IDEA AHEAD

9. After thirty minutes to an hour you should have a fully grown beard of bees (see Fig. 19b).

10. To disperse the bees, hold a large funnel near your face, one with a bottom opening about the size of a soup can. Place the bottom of the funnel into a bag, box, or beehive and give a sudden jerk of your face and body: most of the bees fall right off, but some stragglers may sting you.

DANGER: Depending on the kind of bees used and the daredevil's reaction to bee stings, this stunt could land you in a hospital—or, worse, a morgue.

Chapter 20

WRESTLING AN ALLIGATOR

At just sixteen years old, Robert Jadin started working as a wrestler at one of the dozens of tourist attractions in Florida that offer close-up views of alligators. He soon established a reputation for his instinctual know-how as an alligator wrestler. Jadin was bitten just once while working and suffered only a minor injury to his finger, but he witnessed worse mishaps by other wrestlers who made small mistakes. He recalls the most commonly asked question from the audience while doing a show as, "Why isn't he attacking you and trying to kill and eat you?" The answer was (and is) that alligators are defensive creatures who generally bite only when the wrestler makes a mistake, like putting his hands in the wrong places or becoming complacent.

GATOR GRAPPLERS

Alligator wrestling goes way back. Seminole Indians were experts at taking down the mammoth reptiles for their meat. Later, the activity became sport for a booming tourist industry in Florida. When boosters began to aggressively market the state as a visitor's paradise, alligator wrestling became just another exotic part of the attraction.

Now twenty-two and a biology student at Northeastern State University in Oklahoma, Jadin plans on specializing in the study of venomous snakes and crocodilians. Two years gone from his old job, Jadin's education and maturing appreciation for ecology has turned him into an avid conservationist who believes alligator wrestling for sport should be banned. But the young man remembers

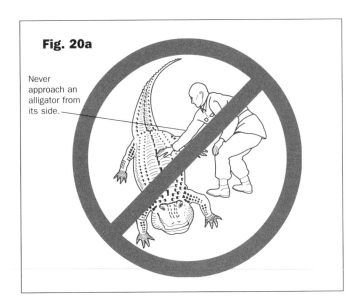

Fig. 20a

Never approach an alligator from its side.

the tricks of the daring trade as if he'd performed them yesterday—and offers some choice advice to would-be wrestlers.

First and foremost, he warns that alligator wrestling can be a brutally dangerous activity with sometimes nasty results: "There are three ways that an alligator can bite a person. They can snap and release really quick, which doesn't cause that bad of a wound and is by far the most common way of being injured; they can hold on and shake their head, very bad for anything inside its mouth; or they can hold on and roll, which is by far the worst."

"Alligators cannot see directly in front or behind them, so don't approach from the side or you'll get bit quick. And don't let size fool you: six-foot gators are more likely to bite you than eight-foot gators, and both have the potential to maim you. But in general gators have pretty small brains, so it's not too hard to predict how they will react to certain situations, and as long as you stay with the same comfortable routine you should be fine," Jadin says. "Alligators have extremely powerful jaws and that is their most dangerous asset—but once their jaws are clamped safely shut, it's really hard for them to open

FLIRTING WITH DISASTER: A HAND IN OPEN JAWS

An alligator cannot see well directly in front of it. With relative ease but serious risk, you can tap the top of a gator's mouth, causing the jaws to open, and then place a hand inside the gaping mouth without the gator knowing the hand is even there. But one inadvertent contact with the gator's tongue, teeth, or nerves—a droplet of sweat, for example—will trigger those powerful snapping jaws faster than you can blink.

their mouths back up. They have incredible closing pressure in their jaws that no man could open if he were to get his hand stuck in. But you can actually keep an eight-foot alligator's mouth closed with one hand because the pressure isn't great in opening."

Wild alligators generally don't want to be bothered, so they will usually swim away in fear unless they've been too conditioned to the presence of humans. The real trick for the would-be alligator wrestler is in abandoning fear and not making mistakes.

HOW THE DAREDEVIL DOES IT

These instructions are for reading entertainment only. They are not to be followed, nor do they convey the full extent of knowledge and training required to attempt these dangerous acts.

Checklist: one eight-foot alligator in a shallow, semi-enclosed body of water; fellow experts

1. Focus on the alligator, and be sure it isn't surrounded by friends.

2. Position yourself to grab the gator's tail. Use a wooden stick if necessary to straighten the tail out.

3. Carefully drag the gator by the tail—or lightly prod the gator along, tapping the stick at its back legs—to an open area where you can work.

4. Approach the gator from behind, jump on its back,

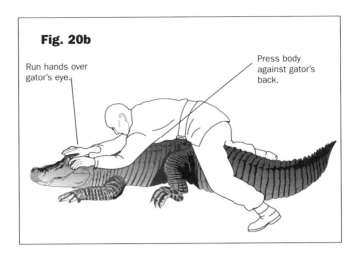

Fig. 20b

Run hands over gator's eye.

Press body against gator's back.

and keep your body firmly pressed against it (see Fig. 20b).

5. Quickly grab the gator's neck, making sure your hands don't get too close to the gator's teeth; its mouth may swing wildly open and around in resistance.

6. In smooth, fluid motions, run your hands over the gator's eyes, push its jaws down, and clamp the jaws shut between your hands and the dirt.

7. Once the gator is still, reach around with one hand and grasp underneath the lower jaw. Use both hands to secure the jaws in a shut position.

DANGER: An adult alligator's clamped jaw can exert more than 2,000 pounds of pressure, which can inflict severe damage on the human body. An alligator can easily sink its teeth completely through a human appendage, rendering permanent damage, disfigurement, and death.

Chapter 21

HOLDING LIVE RATTLESNAKES IN THE MOUTH

O riginally from Rising Star, Texas, Jackie Bibby now lives in another Lone Star town, Whiskey Flats. He has always been intrigued by the rattlesnakes of the Southwest, and became interested in competitive snake handling when he first participated in a rattlesnake roundup at eighteen. "Rattlesnakes only strike at two things: food and fear," Bibby warns in his rapid-fire rural brogue. "You're too big for them to eat, so you'd better not scare 'em."

YIELD
TO CRAZY PEOPLE DOING THIS STUNT

SNAKE, RATTLE, AND ROLL

While most snakes are harmless, the entire lot has suffered from a bad rap stretching far back in history—indeed, to man's biblical beginnings in the Garden of Eden. Few creatures instill as much fear in humans as the serpent. Whether the phobia is linked to the story of Adam and Eve or to some deeper, more inextricable psychic phenomenon, millions of people are profoundly fearful of snakes. One recent report links the fear to a symptom of evolution, a Darwinian throwback to a time when early mammals struggled for survival in a world dominated by reptiles. Today, those who have shed this apparently natural fear may seem almost superhuman to those who have not. Furthermore, when the fearless willfully confront those snake species known to be venomous, they merit the moniker, "daredevil."

Now, thirty-six years and six snakebites wiser, Bibby is still deeply enamored of the serpentine world. He holds the world record for sitting in a bathtub with the most live snakes: eighty-one western diamondbacks. He has squeezed himself into a sleeping bag with 109 live rattlesnakes, breaking another of his own records. He also recently broke his own record by suspending nine live rattlesnakes by their tails in his mouth. "I have to break my own records," Bibby told the *Fort Worth Star Telegram* following his latest feat. "Heck, there's nobody else who can do it."

Of course, the skill of the seasoned snake handler is required, but the real "trick" in getting the most snakes in your mouth is to have their rattles bundled tightly together.

Fig. 21a

Firm grip just below rattle

HOW THE DAREDEVIL DOES IT

These instructions are for reading entertainment only. They are not to be followed, nor do they convey the full extent of knowledge and training required to attempt these dangerous acts.

Checklist: live rattlesnakes; one or two assistants; first-aid kit

1. Have assistants hand snakes to you slowly, one at a time.

2. Hold each snake firmly with the head hanging toward the ground and the rattle just above your fist (see Fig. 21a).

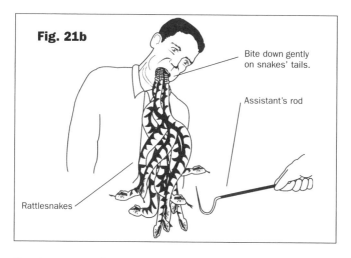

Fig. 21b

Bite down gently on snakes' tails.

Assistant's rod

Rattlesnakes

3. As new snakes are added, keep their tails bundled together tightly with your fist.

4. If one or more of the snakes begins to climb up its own or another snake's body or shows signs of agitation, your assistants should use rods to tap the serpent's head back down.

5. After nine or more snakes are bundled, gently place their rattles into your mouth, bite down gingerly, and hold them suspended for ten seconds (see Fig. 21b).

DANGER: A rattlesnake bite can be painful even if no venom is injected, in what is called a "dry bite" and can also lead to serious infection. If the bite does yield venom, a range of frightening symptoms may follow: swelling, pain, nausea, vomiting, sweating, chills, dizziness, weakness, numbness or tingling of the mouth or tongue, and abnormal heart rate and blood pressure. All bites should be medically treated as soon as possible.

Chapter 22

EATING A LIVE SCORPION

According to a book called *Man Eating Bugs: The Art and Science of Eating Insects,* insects have been providing human beings with sustenance for eons. The book's fifty-six-year-old coauthor Peter Menzel, who lives in Napa, California, is one such human. After an eight-year global bug-eating tour, Menzel, along with his wife, Faith D'Aluisio, wrote the book, one of the world's foremost accounts of entomophagy, which, derived from the Greek, means the eating of insects. Theirs is an account in pictures and words of the couple's bug-eating journeys around the world—from Thailand, China, Indonesia, and Cambodia to Mexico, Venezuela, Peru, and the United States; then off to Australia, South Africa, Uganda, and Botswana.

"WAITER, THERE IS NOT A BUG ON MY PLATE!"

Eating live poisonous insects is hardly a new fad. In fact, it far outdates reality competition TV shows, the South Beach Diet, or even the attention-deprived kid from elementary school. Bugs have been part of the human diet for ages. So it's not surprising that a husband and wife team of American photojournalists traveled the globe, and developed a taste for insects along the way.

During his travels, Menzel and his wife have munched witchetty grubs and honeypot ants in Australia, enormous water bugs, leaping crickets, and tarantulas in Thailand, dragonflies and giant grubs in Indonesia, mealworms in Mexico, and scorpions in China. Of scorpions, Menzel and his bug-eating wife say that

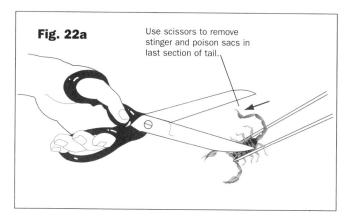

Fig. 22a

Use scissors to remove stinger and poison sacs in last section of tail.

their danger to humans may be exaggerated. There are many species, but only a few that can be considered really dangerous. In most cases, scorpion stings can bring on swelling, pain, and discoloration at the point of the sting. Effects can also include nausea and vomiting. Most symptoms usually subside in twenty-four hours.

"When scorpions are eaten raw, the chef must remove the stingers and venom sacs because the stingers are extremely sharp and the toxins could be absorbed through the mucosal membranes. Cooked scorpions are not devenomed, probably because the small proteins that comprise the toxin are broken down by the heat of cooking."

And what is it like to eat live scorpions? They are crunchy, with chewy, gutsy meat, and a fishy taste. In fact, the flavor is not unlike that of shrimp. And according to Menzel, "After the first live one, it's easy."

HOW THE DAREDEVIL DOES IT

These instructions are for reading entertainment only. They are not to be followed, nor do they convey the full extent of knowledge and training required to attempt these dangerous acts.

Checklist: prongs or chopsticks; rice wine; a scorpion or two

1. Purchase one or two live scorpions from an Asian or exotic-foods store.

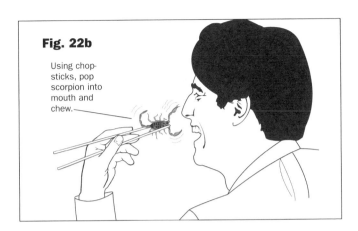

Fig. 22b

Using chopsticks, pop scorpion into mouth and chew.

2. Put the scorpions in a bowl of water. They will thrash around and become very active.

3. Using a spoon, prongs, or chopsticks, take the scorpions out of the water and drop them into a bowl of rice wine, making sure they are thoroughly covered. The wine will put the scorpions into a comalike state and cause them to stop struggling.

4. Using prongs or chopsticks, pick the scorpions out of the wine.

5. Using a pair of scissors, snip off the stingers at the tip of their tails, along with the nearby poison sacs (see Fig. 22a).

6. Discard the stingers and sacs.

7. Pop the scorpion into your mouth (see Fig. 22b) and chew. Enjoy.

DANGER: Severe cases of scorpion toxicity include anxiety and agitation, acute pain at the site of the sting, excessive salivation and perspiration, irregular pulse, unstable body temperature, twitching, and difficulty breathing.

Chapter 23

RIDING A 2,000-POUND RAGING BULL

At five feet eight inches tall and weighing only 150 pounds, John "Cowboy" Hall (also a motorcycle daredevil, see page 136) fits the bill for a bull rider: he's stocky and strong with a low center of gravity, and he was born with an almost insane lack of fear.

RIDING OF THE BULLS

The rodeo is an arena for the ultimate test of man (or woman) versus beast. Bull riding is, bar none, the most dangerous of the many forms of rodeo competition. The bull, often weighing in excess of 2,000 pounds, is none too pleased to be at the rodeo, for one thing. Plus, he instinctively and furiously understands his purpose—to get the cowboy off his back, by any means necessary.

Hall was raised by a number of stepfathers, four of whom were rodeo riders. Following in their boot steps, Hall started riding bulls when he was fifteen. By the time he was nineteen, he was touring the rodeo circuits with the sports' best riders. He rode bulls for thirteen years, often hitchhiking hundreds of miles to get to the rodeos in which he would perform. "It was a different era," says Hall, "before you could really make a ton of money from sponsorships and whatnot."

He was voted the 1966 Arizona state champ for bull riding at the ripe age of twenty-four. "Riding bulls is all about attitude," he says. "Attitude and confidence: some days you feel like you can do anything; others you feel like a piece of crap who can't find himself out of a paper bag."

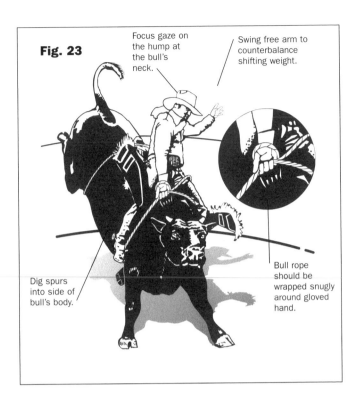

Fig. 23

Focus gaze on the hump at the bull's neck.

Swing free arm to counterbalance shifting weight.

Dig spurs into side of bull's body.

Bull rope should be wrapped snugly around gloved hand.

Regardless of his confidence level, every time Hall found himself on the back of a massive bull, he was risking life and limb. "Riding is like being in a car wreck with the car spinning this way and that," he says. "You cannot easily predict what direction the bull is gonna try throwing you. The bulls are smart and pissed off and they'll try to fake you out."

The equipment used for riding a bull is really quite simple: a rope (called the bull rope) is wrapped tightly around the bull, behind his front legs, and threaded through a loose loop at the end. The rope is knotted in a braided handhold at the bull's shoulders, and is some-times reinforced with leather to make the grip stiffer. A metal bell hangs where the rope is looped, directly underneath the bull, providing a weight so that when the rider is thrown or dismounts, the rope will easily slide off and can be retrieved. The bell also alerts people in the arena that a ride is underway.

HOW THE DAREDEVIL DOES IT

Checklist: rodeo arena; angry, 2,000-pound bull; bull rope; leather riding glove; rosin (pine sap); boots and spurs; judges and rodeo clowns; assistant

1. While it is still in the chute, slide down onto the bull, keeping your toes pointed down so your spurs don't scrape it.

2. Put a leather riding glove on, rubbed with rosin (pine sap) to make your grip sticky, and put your hand through the braided handhold.

3. Have your assistant grab the end of the bull rope and wrap it snugly around your gloved hand, then grip the rope.

4. Put your rope hand alongside the bull's backbone, gripping a pocket of loose hide for extra stability.

5. When the chute is opened and the bull starts bucking, point your toes out and dig your spurs into the side's of the bull.

6. As the bull jerks and bucks, stay focused on the hump at the bull's neck, not on its head, which the bull may move and manipulate in an effort to fake out the rider. If your bull has no hump, focus on its hide about six inches in front of your hand.

7. Swing your free arm like a gyroscope to help counterbalance your shifting weight. Remember not to let your free arm touch the bull, per rodeo regulations.

8. Each time the bull hits the ground, your feet will pop off the bull's side; immediately move them forward and plant them in against the bull, pulling yourself

RIDING A 2,000-POUND RAGING BULL

forward with your spurs and your grip. Try to stay as close to the rope as possible, jumping toward the rope with your body to maintain your center of gravity. (See Fig. 23.)

9. A bull ride lasts eight seconds; if you last that long, your next challenge is getting off.

10. When the whistle blows, slide your hand out of the braided handhold and jerk the rope straight up.

11. Wait for the bull to turn right, preferably, then throw your right leg over to the bull's left side while releasing your grip hand and jumping off, trying to land on your feet.

12. Run the heck away as the rodeo clowns distract the bull and take the heat off you.

DANGER: There is one significant advantage that a human has over a bull: a larger brain. But the bull has many other advantages, including four legs he won't mind using to stomp a human, two horns he won't mind using to skewer a human, and a body mass that may be ten to fifteen times that of a human's. Bull riding is extremely dangerous and the sport has seen many expert riders trampled, maimed, and killed beneath the weight of an angry bull.

IV.

THE
RAZOR'S
EDGE

Chapter 24

THROWING KNIVES AROUND THE SILHOUETTE OF A BEAUTIFUL WOMAN

When the debonair fifty-seven-year-old Reverend Dr. David R. Adamovich, of Freeport, New York, is not sanctifying weddings or conducting funeral ceremonies, he's often found throwing knives around scantily clad female targets. The reverend just happens to be known as The Great Throwdini, the world's foremost knife thrower.

SHARP SHOOTER

Throwing knives around a human target is one of the most perilous acts of the impalement arts. It is a dangerous and double-edged dare that requires two bold individuals: an accomplished and focused thrower, and a brave assistant, who raises the audience's suspense level by submitting herself to potential death.

Adamovich is a world-champion knife thrower who holds a record for the fastest knife throws. He also has authored a comprehensive scientific document on knife throwing, *A Treatise on the Art and Science of Knife Throwing*.

Surprisingly, Adamovich's passion for his art has not been a lifelong interest. He threw his first knife at the age of fifty, when a friend he shot pool with challenged him to toss a knife at a tree. Adamovich's first throw

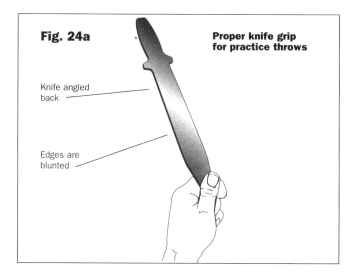

Fig. 24a

**Proper knife grip
for practice throws**

Knife angled
back

Edges are
blunted

was a perfect one, and he was instantly hooked. Since
then, the reverend/knife thrower has been sharpening
his skills religiously. After five years of competition
throwing and several world-championship titles, he developed the confidence necessary to face his greatest fear:
throwing a knife toward—or, rather, around—another
human being. "This is by far the scariest thing I have
ever done. And it is still scary," he says. "It's never an
easy throw when you know that if you screw up, someone's life may be at stake."

Fortunately, Adamovich has never missed in thousands
of throws around assistants. In his act, he also cuts
objects held by his assistant. "I burst balloons with an
ax and cut a straw from my assistant's mouth with a sixteen-inch knife, just inches from her nose." There have
been, he admits, a few mishaps, such as assistants
being knocked with the handles of bounced knives.
Luckily, he has never seriously injured any of his "target
girls" (as assistants are sometimes called).

To aspiring knife throwers, Adamovich recommends years
of training and practice. To begin, he says, start with a
set of three to five throwing knives, preferably fourteen
inches in length from end to end. Generally speaking, a
throwing knife is either single- or double-edged.

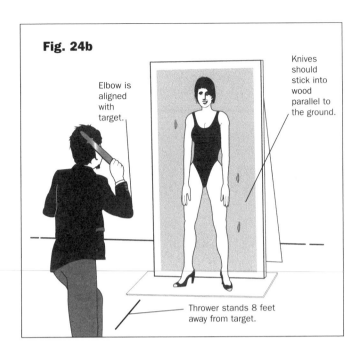

Fig. 24b

Elbow is aligned with target.

Knives should stick into wood parallel to the ground.

Thrower stands 8 feet away from target.

Approximately one-third to one-half of its length has blunted cutting edges, but to stick well in the wood, the knife should have a sharp point. Knives less than twelve inches or more than sixteen inches in total length are more difficult to throw, Adamovich says.

To practice, begin by throwing the knife while holding it by the blade, then work up to throwing it from the handle. When thrown properly, the knife will stick straight out from the wood, parallel to the ground. Then practice like crazy until you have enough control to throw knives around the silhouette of a beautiful woman.

HOW THE DAREDEVIL DOES IT

These instructions are for reading entertainment only. They are not to be followed, nor do they convey the full extent of knowledge and training required to attempt these dangerous acts.

Checklist: throwing knives; large plank of wood (impalement board); assistant

1. Set up your plank of wood and stand approximately eight feet away.
2. Hold the knife by the blade end in your dominant

hand (the handle is angled behind you toward the sky). The edges of a throwing knife are blunted and won't cut you if held properly (see Fig. 24a).

3. Place your opposite foot at the toe line. (If you are right handed, put your left toe at the line.)

4. Holding the knife by the blade, bring it overhead and align the elbow with the target (see Fig. 24b). Then throw the knife toward the target, as if you were throwing a baseball, and as your forearm begins to straighten, release the knife, which should make a half-spin turn before hitting the plank. The knife will stick in the wood, fall to the ground, or bounce back at you.

5. Try to stick the knife in the wood so that it is parallel to the ground: if the handle points skyward, move up a shoe length; if the handle droops down, move back—a shoe length at a time.

6. Once you are able to stick the knife by throwing it from the blade, move back to twelve feet from the target and begin again by throwing the knife from the handle. With this grip, the knife will make one complete spin before sticking in the target.

7. To gain proficiency in throwing knives around a human assistant, place a mannequin in front of the impalement board. Then throw thousands of knives in different patterns around the figure of the woman, from bottom to top and alternating left to right.

8. After you are 100 percent confident that you are good enough to attempt the real thing . . . start shopping for an assistant!

DANGER: When throwing knives, there is always the risk of manslaughter.

Chapter 25

SWALLOWING A SWORD

Sword swallowing is one of the more dignified of timeless dares, an amazing mix of tradition, physiological achievement, and the delicious threat—and apparent defiance—of pain. It is extremely dangerous, so dangerous, in fact, that the *Guinness Book of World Records* stopped recording any such activities—presumably so as not to encourage them.

As with humanity, sword swallowers fall into two categories: the fraudulent and the real deal. The frauds may call themselves sword swallowers but only present the illusion (through sleight of hand or by collapsible swords) of swallowing the entire blade of a sword. Genuine sword swallowers are trained in the ancient art, which dates as far back as Babylonian times, and the most recent tally of authentic masters totaled less than one hundred individuals.

Unfortunately, the phonies do the disservice of creating doubts as to the legitimacy of the genuine performers.

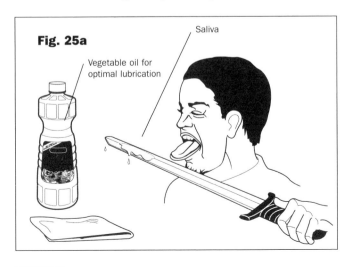

Fig. 25a

Saliva

Vegetable oil for optimal lubrication

To diminish any lingering skepticism and to establish standards, twenty-six-year-old Dai Andrews of Baltimore, Maryland—one of the authentic performers—defines "sword swallowing" as "the act of inserting a solid metal blade at least 15 inches long into the mouth, over the tongue, down the throat, past the vocal cords and epiglottis, down the esophagus, past the heart and lungs, through the esophageal sphincter, and into the stomach."

Furthermore, he goes by the following definition for the sword itself: "a weapon with a nonfolding, nonretractable solid steel or metal blade at least 1/2 inch in width and 15 inches to 20 inches in length, and not recommended to exceed 24 inches in length except in extreme circumstances for performance purposes."

STOP THIS MADNESS

The feats of Andrews amaze even fellow sword swallowers. In addition to presenting the standard challenges of swallowing a straight sword, he claims to have mastered the acutely hazardous curved-blade stunt that requires its performer to bend his body with the blade.

A DIET OF STAINLESS STEEL

One of the first things an aspiring sword swallower must learn is to overcome the gag reflex triggered when an object hits the back of the throat. Similarly, the pharynx, another point that registers sharp and reflexive pain, must be conditioned. Finally, the stomach must be trained to receive foreign objects. All of this requires a preternatural awareness of posture and a pinpoint sense of the location of the sword as it passes through the mouth, throat, and torso. Sword swallowing is a treacherous test of body and mind.

A sideshow performer extraordinaire and adept at a variety of bizarre feats, Andrews is devoted to sword swallowing and undaunted by potentially serious injuries such as internal bruising. He has suffered injuries that

BE THE STUNT

According to Andrews, the mind and the body must unite in a meditative state to perform a successful sword swallow. Andrews recommends the regular practice of yoga or tai chi as a preliminary exercise.

required medical attention, he has experienced abrasions that made eating solid food difficult for a week afterward, and he has had false alarms. (Once, while in Europe, he pulled a sword from his throat after a street performance to find what appeared to be blood on the blade. Only after a panicked search for a hospital did he realize it was just some hot chocolate he had drunk.)

Today Andrews has a lot to brag about, including a regular gig for Carnival Cruise Lines, a history of phenomenal success in Europe, and an appearance in an MTV music video by the band Nello y la Banda del Zoco. But while Andrews is as pro as one can go, his success wasn't instantaneous. "It took me about two and a half years to

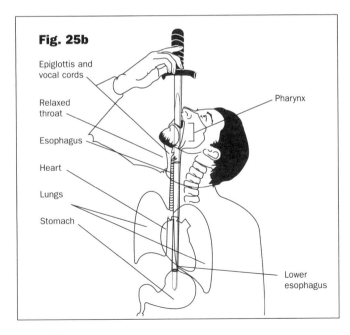

Fig. 25b

Epiglottis and vocal cords

Relaxed throat

Esophagus

Heart

Lungs

Stomach

Pharynx

Lower esophagus

develop any real degree of proficiency," he says. Today, he continues to swallow twelve-inch daggers to the hilt and twenty-four-inch swords before crowds silenced by fear, awe, and disbelief.

HOW THE DAREDEVIL DOES IT

These instructions are for reading entertainment only. They are not to be followed, nor do they convey the full extent of knowledge and training required to attempt these dangerous acts.

Checklist: Sword; olive oil (optional)

1. Lick the blade or coat it with a palatable lubricant like olive oil (see Fig. 26a). (It's also best to refrain from eating sticky foods just prior to performing the stunt.)

2. Stand extremely straight without tensing the muscles of the body.

3. Relax the throat.

4. Raise your chin and slide the sword down with the blade flat against the surface of the tongue.

5. Navigate slowly and steadily through the internal organs (see Fig. 26b). While perfect posture is ideal, minor corrections may be required as the blade slides down.

6. You have a limited time to keep the sword down before your body begins to react, so once the blade is in, remain calm and quickly accentuate the feat with a flourish of your free hand.

7. Carefully remove the sword.

DANGER: It is not difficult to scrape or even puncture vital internal organs while swallowing swords.

Chapter 26

WALKING ON BROKEN GLASS

Thirty-two-year-old Erik Sprague tours the country to perform sideshow stunts. He is known professionally as the Lizardman. (See page 28.) Modified with piercings and scarification, his body is tattooed from head to toe in green, reptilian-like scales. His talents, however, are much more than skin-deep. His résumé is long and his abilities are wide-ranging, including a mastery of walking barefoot over broken glass. In fact, to really give his audience a show of his extraordinary daring, he often ends his broken glass walk routine with a good amount of shard-stomping insanity.

BROKEN GLASS BOOGIE WALK

Ever stub a toe or snag a splinter in your foot? Those mishaps will seem minute after seeing a daredevil cakewalk barefoot over a floor layered with broken liquor bottles. This "feat" is a veritable promenade of physical and mental conditioning honed to waltzlike perfection. It is a dance with pain, and those who do it well make it look oh-so-easy.

Sprague credits his fearlessness simply to a matter of practice, and he likens the stunt to boxing: "When you get jabbed the first time, you feel stunned, but after a while it barely fazes you. You've learned to take the hits and go in for the body shot."

Of course, Sprague has taken hits. He has been cut many times, but fortunately never too severely. He has seen others have their feet pierced by large shards, requiring serious emergency medical attention. He

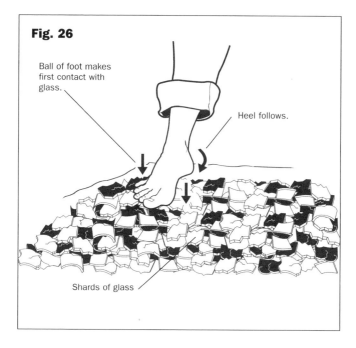

Fig. 26

Ball of foot makes first contact with glass.

Heel follows.

Shards of glass

warns: "If you're considering showing off by walking on broken glass, also consider how cool you may look having to limp for eight months."

The chance of injury is just that: chance. There is no way around it. "Many people can have successful glass walks after only brief preparation," says Sprague. "However, this does not mean that the next time they attempt they won't fail. Glass never breaks the same way twice, and along with many other unpredictable variables, that makes this a very dangerous act. Over time, if you do it enough, you are guaranteed a serious cut by the sheer statistical weight. Mastering walking on broken glass is hard to judge because you may do it once or a thousand times perfectly and then get badly hurt the next time—it's unpredictable."

No specific training is necessary, but conditioning the soles of the feet and developing thick calluses can make for a much better glass-walking experience. Sprague suggests spending a lot of time walking around on bare feet. It is also imperative to use clean glass, a flat surface, and dry feet.

The rest is mental. The main thing to keep in mind, Sprague says, is that glass can always cut. You must stay focused, he warns, while keeping in the forefront of your mind a realistic perception and respect for the danger. "It's when you let your guard down that you get hurt," he says.

HOW THE DAREDEVIL DOES IT

These instructions are for reading entertainment only. They are not to be followed, nor do they convey the full extent of knowledge and training required to attempt these dangerous acts.

Checklist: clean bottles; heavy canvas or burlap sack to smash the bottles in; a hammer to smash the bottles; flat surface; dry feet

1. Put a large number of thick bottles in the sack and smash them up. (Thin, small bottles make smaller, thinner shards, which don't look as good on stage or break as nicely.)

2. Remove any unbroken bottlenecks.

3. Lay the shards evenly on a flat, dry surface. Don't layer the shards too thickly or it may be harder to keep your balance; too thinly and it won't be that impressive.

4. Put one foot onto the carpet of glass, ball of foot first (see Fig. 26).

5. Keep your toes curled back and up.

6. Gradually apply your weight and roll the foot down onto the heel.

7. If you feel any immediate sharp pain, lift the foot back up. (It helps to have something or someone to lean on, such as an assistant, since you may need to stand on one foot at times to clear glass off your sole.)

8. Once one foot is on the glass, repeat with the other, and then walk toe-to-heel across the glass, following the above procedure.

DANGER: One of the hidden dangers in the broken glass walk is the possibility of slipping and falling, which can lead to serious cuts. The glass should not be layered too thickly or balance may become tricky.

Chapter 27

LYING BETWEEN TWO BEDS OF NAILS BENEATH MORE THAN 1,500 POUNDS

As owner of Graber's Academy of Martial Arts and Fitness Center in Akron, Ohio, thirty-nine-year-old Lee Graber's work is rigorous and demanding. He's a Midwesterner with strong family values, and grew up like the rest of the kids in his neighborhood—with unblinking admiration for his father. Father knows best, as they say, and like father, like son.

HEAVY METAL NAIL SALON

There are many spin-offs of the age-old bed-of-nails stunt, and one of the most intense is the Iron Maiden: a person lies on top of a bed of nails; another bed of nails is placed on top of the person, nails pointing downward; and, finally, a large amount of weight is placed on top of that, adding enormous pressure through the sharp points of contact pressing upon the body. With a large load bearing down, the daunting sandwich of nails presses painfully upon both front and back. The Iron Maiden is a truly torturous test of endurance.

After watching his father and two other men perform a stunt called the three-man triple bed of nails in which three men are layered, like a club sandwich, between three beds of nails, young Lee himself became fascinated with the bed-of-nails feat. "My father was one of the three men who performed the triple bed of nails in the 1970s, and after seeing him do that I wanted to try it."

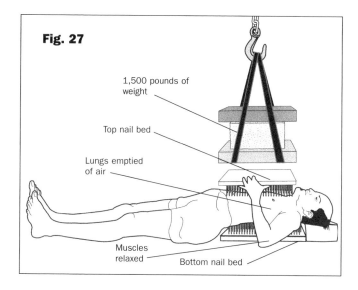

Fig. 27

1,500 pounds of weight

Top nail bed

Lungs emptied of air

Muscles relaxed

Bottom nail bed

A generation later, in 2000, Junior set a world record for withstanding the heaviest Iron Maiden—1,659 pounds—a weight that bore down on him for more than ten seconds. "The Iron Maiden involved me lying down on a bed of nails. Then another bed of nails was placed on my chest with the nails pointing into my chest. Then a crane was used to lift the 1,659 pounds on top of me. After the weight was on me and the chain was released, I had to stay there for ten seconds—it ended up being fifteen seconds [before the weight was removed]. Then the weight was lifted off, and the top bed of nails was lifted off, and I was lifted up off of the nails. I then removed my shirt to show that I had hundreds of nail marks in my back and chest. But no puncture holes, no blood!"

Unfortunately, Graber's dad, who passed away in 1998, wasn't around to see his son's amazing achievement. But his son still garners emotional and mental strength from his father. Before performing such feats, Graber says he needs some solitude. "I go somewhere where I can be alone, and I focus on slowing down my breathing and heart rate. I do this by meditation. Then I ask my father for his help. Then I ask God to help me through it." It, understandably, is no easy ordeal, and failing the Iron

MAKING THE BED YOU LIE IN

Buy a piece of plywood that adequately spans your shoulders in width and the distance from your shoulders to your waist in length. Put the board on a couple of sawhorses. Pre-drill hundreds of evenly-spaced holes throughout the plywood with a drill bit slightly smaller in diameter than the nails, so the nails fit snugly in the plywood. Hammer very sharp three-inch framing nails into the holes. The number of nails depends on your experience and your ambition. "I use roughly 250 on each bed," says Graber. "I make my beds with fewer nails than a lot of people. Some people use a thousand nails. The fewer the nails, the more difficult it is to lie on them. That's because there are fewer nails to take the weight, which means there is more body pressure on each nail."

Maiden can turn you into a human shish kebab. Graber only performed the Iron Maiden once, when he set the record, during which time the pressure of the weight ruptured some blood vessels in his eye and his shoulder. Graber has set other bed-of-nails records: for enduring a bed of nails with five people stacked on top of each other, all lying on their own beds of nails; and for enduring the most concrete blocks broken by a sledgehammer (thirty-four) while lying on a bed of nails.

HOW THE DAREDEVIL DOES IT

These instructions are for reading entertainment only. They are not to be followed, nor do they convey the full extent of knowledge and training required to attempt these dangerous acts.

Checklist: two beds of nails; more than 1,500 pounds of weight; crane with a pulley system; crane operator; several trusty assistants

1. Focus on controlling your breathing and slowing down your heart rate.

2. Lie down on the bottom bed of nails.

3. Have the other bed of nails placed on top of you, flat and balanced.

4. Have the crane operator lift the weights. Before the weight is placed on top of you, push all of the air out of your lungs by exhaling in short, rapid bursts. Relax your muscles (see Fig. 27).

5. Have the crane operator gently place the weights on top of the nail bed.

6. Do not resist the weight as it is placed on top of you.

7. Keep the air pushed out of your lungs, and try not to constrict your muscles too tightly.

8. Have your assistants disconnect the weight from the crane. Maintain the weight for as long as you can, probably no more than ten seconds.

9. Expect to feel a tingling, pinching sensation as you lie on the nails, but do not try to reposition yourself in an attempt to relieve this sensation. If you drag your body along the bed, you could easily scrape and rip your skin.

10. Have the crane operator remove the weight, then have your assistants remove the top bed of nails.

11. When the top bed of nails is removed, breathe calmly. Then have your assistants lift you from the bottom bed of nails.

DANGER: Suffocation, blood loss, ruptured blood vessels, crushed organs, broken ribs, death—all are risks of this extremely dangerous dare.

Chapter 28

CATCHING AN ARROW IN MIDFLIGHT WHILE BLINDFOLDED

Terry Bryan is by no measure a target for the public spotlight, nor does he want to be. But in the spring of 2003, the fifty-one-year-old appeared on *Ripley's Believe It or Not!* and caught a speeding arrow in midflight while blindfolded. His performance was intended to demonstrate the almost unbelievable power of mental discipline

MARTIAL ARCHERY

Humanity is graced with the ability to embrace a variety of intimate relationships: husband and wife, parent and child, brother and sister, cellmate and cellmate. None of these, however, can touch the level of trust that bonds the archer and the person standing seventy-five feet away from him in front of a target, poised to catch a 135-mph flying dart with bare hands while blindfolded. This stunt speaks to the precision skills of both people involved as well as to a kind of trust very few of us will ever know. For the person catching the arrow, it is also a show of hasty handwork and phenomenal focus.

"I did not do this as a 'stunt,'" says Bryan. "I did it as an example of what the human mind can achieve. There are physical abilities you need—hand speed and stuff. The real key is to say that anything is possible if you put your mind to it. That's what martial arts is. Martial arts is ten percent physical and ninety percent mental."

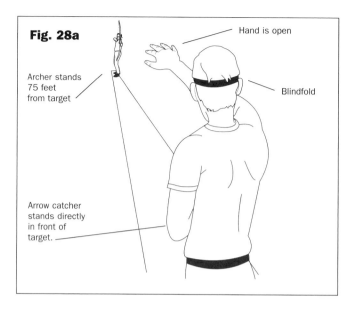

Fig. 28a

Archer stands 75 feet from target

Hand is open

Blindfold

Arrow catcher stands directly in front of target.

Bryan learned martial arts while serving in the U.S. Army in the early 1970s. After a stint in Vietnam, he wondered what he could do with his skills. "I said to myself, 'I'm a trained killer. I can take people out with my hands or an M-16 or with dogs.' … and I decided to teach." Today, Bryan owns American Black Belt Academy in Colorado Springs, Colorado, and uses martial arts to help people—especially kids—gain confidence.

Bryan learned how to catch an arrow specifically for Ripley's. But the program had its own end of the bargain to hold up. According to Bryan, the episode began with a reference from a former martial arts instructor: "My old instructor, Jim Mather, had done this in the mid-1970s for a show called *That's Incredible!* The Ripley's people saw the clip and called him and asked if he could do it for their show. He said, 'Are you crazy, I did that in my fifties, now I'm in my eighties.' He gave them my name and they called me and asked me if I did it, and I said I didn't. I've got a degree in social work and child psychology. We teach karate programs in high schools. We teach kids goal setting. I said I wasn't interested. A few weeks later the Ripley's people called me back and said they would run a piece on the value of martial arts if I did it."

Bryan trained intensively for six weeks with a professional archer the TV show provided for him. On each try, Bryan practiced keeping his starting standing positions identical; the archer's aim, too, had no room for variance. "People have been shot in the neck and have lost their eyes doing this," Bryan said. "If the archer is a half inch off, it can cause me real problems."

A methodology between archer and catcher developed: The archer aims directly at Bryan's left shoulder as they face each other some seventy-five feet apart. Bryan keeps his right arm extended forwarded and ready to intercept the arrow. As the arrow is fired, Bryan rotates his body to the left, and reaches out and grabs the arrow a scant two inches from his body, before it reaches its target. By virtue of his intense training and focus, Bryan's physical responses are triggered almost automatically.

It was a first for Bryan when he performed on the show blindfolded. "I missed the first one and got hit on the arm. A chunk of skin went flying. Then I caught the second one," he says.

It was only on his way to the set that Bryan decided to try the stunt blindfolded. He realized that because he didn't see the arrow flying anyway, he relied solely on his sense of hearing. "I hear the string go twang, and I hear the feathers rushing through the air, and I know where the arrow is going, and that gives me an advantage."

HOW THE DAREDEVIL DOES IT

These instructions are for reading entertainment only. They are not to be followed, nor do they convey the full extent of knowledge and training required to attempt these dangerous acts.

Checklist: highly competent archer; bow and arrow; blindfold; target; total silence

1. Stand blindfolded a few feet in front of the target. Have the archer aim at the very top of your left shoulder, with the target directly behind you, from seventy-five feet away (see Fig. 28a).

Fig. 28b

Left leg pivots back as arrow launches from bow.

Right hand reaches for arrow as it approaches catcher.

2. Remain relaxed, focusing on nothing but sound. Keep your right arm outstretched and your hand open and ready.

3. Upon hearing the arrow launch from the bow, swing your left foot back.

4. As you swing your foot back, simultaneously pivot your body so that you are standing sideways with your right shoulder facing the archer.

5. Keep your hand just out of the line of fire.

6. Listen closely, and when you hear the arrow approaching, thrust out your hand and snatch the arrow from midair with a firm grip (see Fig. 28b).

DANGER: In addition to presenting the risk of getting punctured in the head or vital organs by a sharp arrow, this stunt can easily cause damage to your hands. A grab that is only slightly too fast can result in a hole in the hand, and a grab that is only slightly too slow can cause the arrow's feathers to shred your fingers.

V.

MOTORHEADED MADNESS

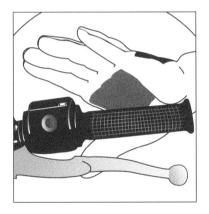

Chapter 29

DOING A WHEELIE ON A MOTORCYCLE AT 100 MILES PER HOUR

Performing as the stunt team d-Aces Street Bike Extreme, twenty-nine-year-old Dan Urban and twenty-six-year-old Cory Kufahl are two motorcycle maniacs who, for the past seven years, have been raising more than just eyebrows and radar detector readings. In addition to performing a host of other tricks, both are masters at the high-speed wheelie, and they can ride with the front wheel in the air for miles on end.

THE DUKES OF HAPHAZARD

Today's motorcycle daredevils are the godchildren of '70s-era stuntman Evel Knievel. Advances in technology have improved bike performance over the years, and there are many schools of stunt riders and professional racers, ranging from off-road competition to the street-racing circuit. One seriously dangerous indicator that a rider has mastered his machine is his ability to do a high-speed wheelie, which requires a refined degree of control, excellent balance, and, of course, daredevil bravado.

The daredevil duo has performed throughout the United States, in Guatemala, and in Jamaica, and they sell videos of their motorized mayhem to fans far and wide. Urban rides a '97 Suzuki GSXR 600; Kufahl rides a '97 Suzuki TL1000. Fortunately, the two men have never suffered any serious injuries—just a few cases of road rash. They have never filed an insurance claim, and they do their own bike maintenance and repairs. It is clear they love what they do.

"Ever since I was a kid I've ridden dirt bikes and bicycles and have been doing stunts. I love doing stunts," says Urban. Kids who love doing stunts on dirt bikes are certainly more likely to inherit the traits of the road-roaring, rubber-burning daredevil, and speed is one such natural compulsion to which driving records speak loudly. According to their Web site, Kufahl has amassed more than eighty tickets since the age of sixteen; Urban, roughly half that number. "I push everything if I'm out driving," says Kufahl. "I know it's stupid, but I like to do it."

In their defense, they report, "We take every ticket to court and usually do well. Very few license suspensions."

Today, skirting the law and capturing it on videotape are among their main entrepreneurial concerns. "No, it is not legal for us to stunt on public roads," their Web site states, "but we do what has to be done to make our videos entertaining and keep raising our skills."

Fig. 29a

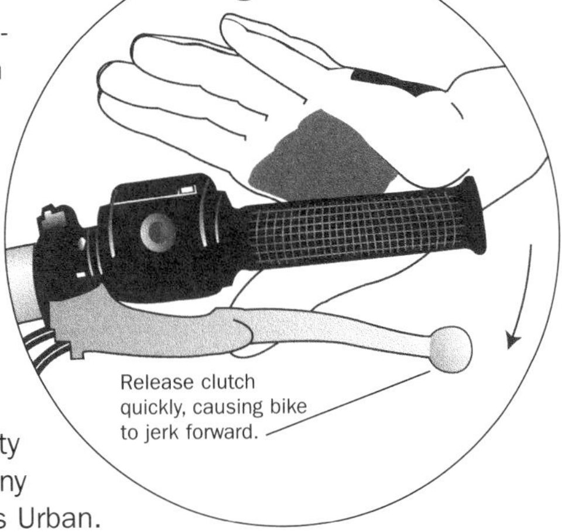

Release clutch quickly, causing bike to jerk forward.

With lots of experience and between 400 and 500 pounds of special stunt bikes under their belts, the pair has learned the fine points of supple riding and smooth throttling. "We can be riding along at about sixty miles per hour—any speed really," says Urban. "You pull in the clutch and let it out quickly—that brings the front end up, and you pull up on the front end, and then you are up in the air. Then you

Fig. 29b

Front wheel lifts off the road.

Weight shifts back.

reach the balance point, and you shift through the gears without using the clutch. But you have to be real smooth on the throttle."

HOW THE DAREDEVIL DOES IT

These instructions are for reading entertainment only. They are not to be followed, nor do they convey the full extent of knowledge and training required to attempt these dangerous acts.

Checklist: a high-performance street motorcycle; protective gear such as helmet, knee pads, shin guards, boots, back protector, and a padded leather jacket; a long, straight, and preferably dead-end road

1. Make sure the road is clear of oil slicks, pebbles, or other possible interferences.

2. Get the motorcycle going to 40–50 mph.

3. Pull in the clutch and let it out quickly so that the bike jerks forward (see Fig. 29a).

4. As it jerks, shift your weight to the back of the bike and lift the front end into the air without tipping the bike back too far (see Fig. 29b).

5. Meanwhile, increase the speed very smoothly.

6. Without using the clutch, shift gears while speeding up. (Bikes can easily be shifted without using the clutch once the proper RPM is reached. All bikes have tachometers; when the RPMs hit four or five thousand, just shift into the next gear using the gear shift lever manipulated by your left foot.)

7. Speed up to 100 mph.

8. Decrease speed to stop the wheelie.

DANGER: Motorcycle riders always run the risk of serious accidents. This danger increases with the riding behaviors of the daredevil biker.

Chapter 30

DOING A "STOPPIE" ON A MOTORCYCLE AT 100 MILES PER HOUR

Wisconsin-based daredevils Dan Urban and Cory Kufahl have perfected the stoppie, and they can roll with their back tires in the air for over 500 feet. It is an extremely difficult and dangerous trick to learn. It takes time, training, strength, and an intimate knowledge of the bike's weight and balance requirements.

RAISING HELL ON FRONT WHEELS

High-speed "stoppies" involve engaging a bike's front brake so that the back end lifts into the air while the rider maintains a controlled roll on the spinning front wheel. Simply put, it is an extended back-tire wheelie, maintained until the bike rolls itself to a stop.

In his long list of impressive tricks, the stoppie is Cory Kufahl's favorite. He can do a stoppie at 120 mph, but "the road has to be absolutely perfect," he says. He generally does them at 90–100 mph and can easily roll on the front wheel for upwards of 500 feet. Why does he get such a thrill out of flirting with disaster? "It's my nature, I guess."

"The key here is to be smooth on the brake," says co-daredevil Urban. "The front wheel is never really locked up. It took us about a year to become proficient at this one. We started doing stoppies at thirty-five miles per hour, and now do them at a hundred miles per hour. But it takes time to learn. You have to learn to be extremely smooth and put

Fig. 30

Apply brake gradually.

Back tire lifts off the road.

Front tire rolls forward.

the correct amount of pressure on the front brakes."
You also have to learn to balance the bulk of the bike
against its tendency to lean toward one side or another.
This is a very delicate operation that will make the differ-
ence between a well-executed stunt and a wipeout of
bone-shattering magnitude.

"You have to concentrate on keeping the bike straight," says Urban.
"At first you concentrate hard on the
steering, but after a while it
becomes natural—just like riding a
bicycle." Of course, practice makes
perfect, and in this case, there's little room for "almost" perfect.

CROSSING
AHEAD
TO INSANITY

HOW THE DAREDEVIL DOES IT

These instructions are for reading entertainment only. They are not to be followed, nor do they convey the full extent of knowledge and training required to attempt these dangerous acts.

Checklist: a high-performance street motorcycle; protective gear such as helmet, knee pads, shin guards, boots, back protector, and a padded leather jacket; a long, straight, and preferably dead-end road

1. Get the bike going up to 100 mph.

2. Very carefully apply pressure to the front brake and feel as the weight of the bike gradually transfers to the front tire.

3. Continue to apply pressure gradually until the back tire lifts off the ground.

4. Keep the pressure applied in such a way as to maintain the lift of the back tire as the front wheel continues rolling forward (see Fig. 30).

5. Use your body to control the back end of the bike, as it will tend to lean toward one side or the other.

6. Use your lower body strength to keep the back in line and your upper body strength to steer the bike straight.

DANGER: In addition to the danger inherent in riding a motorcycle at high speeds, the stoppie presents the additional risk of a heavy bike flipping on top of you with a potentially fatal impact.

DOING A "STOPPIE" ON A MOTORCYCLE AT 100 MILES PER HOUR

Chapter 31

DRIVING IN A DEMOLITION DERBY

"**T**here ain't really much to understand," Ed Jager once told the *New York Times.* "In most motor sports, the winner is the car that finishes first. In demo, it's the car that finishes. You smash things. It don't take a genius."

OFF-ROAD RAGE

The demolition derby provides the ultimate motivation for recycling old cars: psychopathic entertainment. The sport combines an obsession with the automobile with the primal urge to smash it up. The derby's phenomenal popularity springs from the seductive power of destruction: it's hard not to enjoy the spectacle of one of humankind's greatest creations, the automobile, violently transformed into a battering ram in a metal-bashing, mud-spitting, exhaust-spewing furious rage. It's as American as apple pie!

But in the down-and-dirty world of the demolition derby, forty-four-year-old Jager, otherwise known as Speedo, is a genius. One of America's finest demo drivers, Jager has competed in hundreds of derbies; his career is the stuff of legend. He was star and subject of an insightful 2003 documentary titled simply *Speedo,* by film director Jesse Moss.

Speedo, who loved drag racing on city streets, happened quite by chance upon his destiny when one day a buddy asked for help in competing in a demo derby. Speedo wound up winning the very first heat in which he drove.

"It was addictive," Speedo says of that first win, and of the smashing and burning and squealing tires. He was

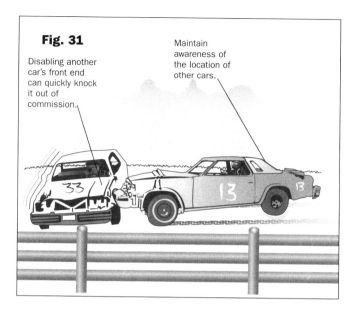

Fig. 31

Disabling another car's front end can quickly knock it out of commission.

Maintain awareness of the location of other cars.

hooked and began entering events at the Flemington Raceway in New Jersey, smashing his way to victory after victory.

"It's a blast, especially when you can bounce off some guy and continue on your way," Speedo says. "It's even better when you hit somebody and see one part of their car go one way and another part go another way, and all you've got is a little bump on your tire."

Demolition derby driving is a wild, brawling sport that often finds fans throwing beer cans and hot dogs at the officials, and the officials throwing beer cans and hot dogs back at the crowd. It is no surprise, then, that Speedo, deemed "too dangerous," became the envy of drivers and officials alike. Speedo likes to slam opponents broadside with the front end of his car. He also likes to hit them head-on. "I was banned for hitting too hard, banned for rough driving, and banned for this and banned for that. But I kept coming back," Speedo says.

Hitting head-on has been part of his success. Most drivers don't do it. But as an experienced auto mechanic, Speedo has studied how cars are built, and he knows that manufacturers build cars to crumble at certain points when they are hit, in order to protect the occupants and the engines. So Speedo strengthens these weak points with metal, special welding techniques, and other tricks, which gives him an edge on the track.

Because Speedo has fortified his front ends, he can run head-on into people without worrying as much as the other drivers. Speedo fondly remembers one national derby: "I did so much damage. I just kept hitting and hitting people. I hit one guy who had a 500-cubic-inch engine, and it blew up in a ball of flames."

Speedo's legendary career was built on blood, sweat, tears, and motor oil. Now, with demo cars piled up in his backyard, Speedo hopes his two sons, twenty-one-year-old Anthony and sixteen-year-old Mike, will follow in their dad's skid marks.

HOW THE DAREDEVIL DOES IT:

These instructions are for reading entertainment only. They are not to be followed, nor do they convey the full extent of knowledge and training required to attempt these dangerous acts.

Checklist: demolition car fixed according to derby regulations

1. Get a junk car, or buy one from a demolition derby expert. (Beginners, especially, should buy the cheapest running car they can find.)

2. Gut the car of anything flammable, including seat covers, rugs, mats, door panels, and other such things.

3. Strengthen the car at the points where it might be weak. (A mechanic can help identify these.)

4. Enter a demolition derby.

5. The cars are either scattered about the track or lined up in rows depending on the venue and the rules. The race starts when the referee gives the signal.

6. Once on the track, stay out of the way of other drivers. You win a demolition derby by being the last car on the track left running, so your strategy is twofold: smash the other cars out of commission, and avoid being smashed yourself. It's a tricky game of hunting while avoiding being hunted.

7. While staying on the defense, go on the attack. Look for opportunities to get a quick "hit" without being caught in the path of an easy attacker.

8. Find a target and smash into it with the idea of trying to disable the car. Common tactics include clear broadside smashes into opponents' front or rear wheels (see Fig. 31) or straight-on backward trunk slams into opponents' front ends.

9. Take advantage of other attacks-in-progress. Attack one of those cars while its driver is distracted. Depending on the positioning of your vehicle, either attack the attacker or double-team the attacked, always keeping the defense of your own vehicle in mind.

10. Make sure yours is the last car running on the track.

DANGER: Whiplash is one of the more common symptoms of the regular demolition derby driver, but there are far worse consequences to entering an automotive arena where destruction is the sole object of the game. On a demolition derby course it is not uncommon to find furious fistfights, inebriated drivers, and cars catching fire, all of which can lead to serious injury and/or death.

Chapter 32

JUMPING A MOTORCYCLE THROUGH A WALL OF FIRE

Former bull rider John Hall (see page 99) says he was one of the founding members of the Dirty Dozen, a notorious motorcycle club that, in the late 1960s and early 1970s, was the bane of the Arizona Highway Department. Dirty Dozen Club membership grew far beyond the original twelve to some 2,000 members before the organization disbanded in the mid-1990s. But Hall remembers the good old days; he is one of those unique beings truly "born to be wild."

HALL OF FLAME

A motorcycle says one thing of its rider: I'm bad. A motorcycle that is used for spectacles such as jumping over cars and through walls of flame says a bit more: I'm superbad. The flamboyantly bedecked motorcycle daredevil is an original phenomenon of post–World War II America—and his antics remain a favorite spectator sport today.

"I used to party with Evel [Knievel] quite a bit," Hall says. "We used to go to all the Playboy clubs together. Someone once challenged me to try and break his record of jumping over nineteen cars on a motorcycle. I said, 'Hell, I can do that.' So I jumped over twenty cars at a small track in Nashville. I don't think Evel liked that too much."

As a showman, Hall tried constantly to make his daredevil routine a thing of beauty, a spectacle to behold. He

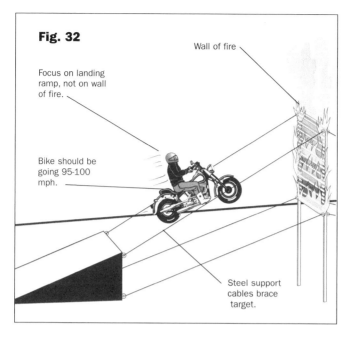

Fig. 32

Wall of fire

Focus on landing ramp, not on wall of fire.

Bike should be going 95-100 mph.

Steel support cables brace target.

says he was the first daredevil to incorporate the wall of fire into a ramp-to-ramp jump, during a motorcycle performance in 1972.

The stunt involved jumping a distance of about 150 feet, from one ramp to another. At the apex of his jump, he would crash through a flaming wall made of one-by-fours and cardboard. "Sometimes," says Hall, "pieces of the wall would stay stuck to me, and when I landed, there would be flames flying off me and my crew would have to use fire extinguishers to put them out."

Today, Hall builds custom motorcycles out of his home in Mesa, Arizona. At sixty-two, he still likes to ride bikes and is a regular pilgrim to some of the larger biker rallies.

For any kind of motorcycle stunt, Hall recommends a lot of practice. "With jumping ramp to ramp," he says, "start small and gradually increase the distance between the ramps. You need to perfect a 150-foot ramp-to-ramp jump to do a decent wall of fire. I think I used to have to get my bike going up to about ninety-five or one hundred miles per hour. But, of course, it also depends on the angles of your ramps."

Before attempting the wall of fire, Hall recommends becoming an expert on ramp jumping. Practice with a short distance between small ramps, and work your way up to longer distances between larger ramps, varying the angles and speeds as you experiment. When you feel confident that you can make any jump, only then should you attempt the wall of fire.

HOW THE DAREDEVIL DOES IT

These instructions are for reading entertainment only. They are not to be followed, nor do they convey the full extent of knowledge and training required to attempt these dangerous acts.

Checklist: two ramps; two tall beams of wood; several eight-foot-long one-by-fours; loose cardboard; steel support cables; five gallons of gasoline; matches; motorcycle; protective gear such as helmet, padded suit, gloves, and boots; trusty crew of assistants; fire extinguishers

1. Practice the 150-foot jump between two ramps until you have perfected it.

2. To build the wall of fire, begin by setting up two tall vertical beams midway between the ramps, about eight feet apart—enough room to fly through comfortably on your jump path.

3. Have a trusty assistant watch you jump between the beams, noting the height where your bottom wheel passes by the beams.

4. Attach a one-by-four horizontally between the beams approximately two feet below this point. About ten feet above the first one-by-four, attach another.

5. Close the gap between the top and bottom with the remaining one-by-fours, leaving small spaces between each plank.

6. Weave a good amount of cardboard into the spaces

between the planks until you have built your makeshift wall.

7. Attach steel support cables from the top and middle of the wall to the top and base of each ramp. This will keep the wall steady and maintain its integrity between the ramps.

8. Have your assistants douse the wall with about five gallons of gasoline, then light it on fire.

9. Don your protective gear and get on your motorcycle. Rev your engine and watch as the flames grow.

10. When the wall is fully engulfed, accelerate toward the first ramp.

11. You should be going 95–100 mph as your bike launches off the first ramp (see Fig. 32). Your focus should be on landing on the second ramp, just as you did in the practice jumps. Try not to be distracted by the wall of fire.

12. As you crash through the flaming wall, maintain your balance and trajectory.

13. Land on the second ramp with your back tire first, immediately following with a smooth front tire landing.

14. Come to a stop within the shortest reasonable distance.

DANGER: Death, broken bones, fractured skull, broken neck, broken back, paralysis, and severe burns—any or all of these are likely outcomes.

Chapter 33

FORMING A SEVEN-PERSON PYRAMID ON A SINGLE MOVING MOTORCYCLE

The twelve women who call themselves "Hardly Angels" are disciples of the daredevil spirit; they formed the first female motorcycle drill team in the United States. Based in Durango, Colorado, this biker-babe outfit currently includes women ranging in age from fifteen to sixty-three. From teenager to senior citizen, the Hardly Angels are bound by their common love of the motorcycle.

STEADY AS SHE GOES

Here's a new take on an old stunt. Most of us know about the old collegiate prank of stuffing dozens of people into a single car. Combine multiple bodies with a single two-wheeled vehicle, add the elements of motion and balance, and you have the makings of a "hawg"-bottomed human pyramid that moves along precariously at up to twenty-five miles per hour, making turns and turning heads.

After marrying a biker and raising kids, 107-pound Lynell Corbett decided it was her turn to rev the chopper's engine. The former elementary school home economics and gymnastics teacher established the group in 1993. "I had seen a lot of [motorcycle] drill teams and realized that there were no women drill teams," she says. "I had experience in gymnastics and some dance, and I thought it would be fun. I figured that if we could choreograph things

Fig. 33

Team members react
in unison to movement
of motorcycle.

Driver maintains speed
of 10-25 mph.

to music and wear costumes, that would be an added
level of entertainment."

"One member is an accountant," she says of her group.
"Others are secretaries and things. Normal people.
We're all just regular gals. Everybody I talked to said,
'You can't do that. Those men have been riding for twen-
ty years.' So we did it."

The Angels devised a spectacular routine centered
around their signature stunt, the Seven-Up, which
involves seven women riding on a single bike while it
travels over 200 yards and makes turns. As Corbett
explains, "One [Angel] is driving. One is standing on the
seat behind the driver. One is standing on the crash
guard on the front of the handlebars. I'm on one side on

one of the running boards with my left foot, and my partner is on the other side with a foot on a running board. Then Dakota, the driver's daughter, sits on the front fender. Another sits on the back luggage rack."

A great burden of the stunt falls upon the driver. "She has to be silky smooth on that clutch," Corbett says. "Anybody who has ever ridden a motorcycle knows that riding slowly is the hardest thing. When you slow down, the bike just wants to fall over. She [the driver] cannot jerk a bit. We are holding on to each other and we are very precariously balanced. The turns are the hard part. Everybody has to lean and we all have to lean at once and the same amount." When riding at speeds between ten and twenty-five miles per hour, the key component to all of the Angels' stunts is balance.

In their dedication to the almighty motorcycle, the members of Hardly Angels have suffered numerous injuries: some have broken collarbones, others have endured bad bruises, sprains, and broken thumbs. But because the members are spread out across the Four Corners area of the Desert Southwest (Utah, Colorado, Arizona, and New Mexico), Corbett says that "the most dangerous part of this gig is getting to and from practices."

SANE PEOPLE
KEEP RIGHT
OF THIS

But get there they do, rain or shine. Even when conditions render driving difficult, these dedicated daredevils practice in parking lots, walking through their routines and memorizing their parts.

HOW THE DAREDEVIL DOES IT

Checklist: seven women; two spotters; one motorcycle

1. With bike running but standing still, assume these positions:
   > one driver
   > one passenger standing on seat behind driver
   > one passenger standing on crash guard on handlebars
   > one passenger standing on one foot on running board on one side
   > one passenger standing on one foot on opposite running board
   > one passenger sitting on front fender
   > one passenger sitting on luggage rack

2. Have the two spotters help the women maintain their positions.

3. The driver releases the clutch very slowly and steadily and the bike starts moving.

4. The women maintain a fluid, balanced group reaction to the motion of the motorcycle as it turns (see Fig. 33).

DANGER: To be silky smooth on the clutch is a challenge of the highest order. One slight jerk and your group goes tumbling over, snapping collarbones, busting thumbs, and creating the risk of a six-hundred-pound metal monster collapsing on top of hundred-pound human frames.

FORMING A SEVEN-PERSON PYRAMID ON A SINGLE MOVING MOTORCYCLE

VI.

FLIGHTS
OF
FANCY

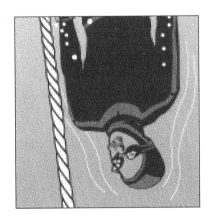

Chapter 34

DIVING HUNDREDS OF FEET UNDERWATER WITHOUT SCUBA EQUIPMENT

Thirty-four-year-old Rudi Castineyra, originally from Cuba, has been training his twenty-four-year-old Turkish wife, Yasemin Dalkilic, since 1999. Between 1999 and 2000, Dalkilic has set six world records in four different categories and has won several prestigious competitions. Falling just short of the 411-foot world record for deepest no-limits free dive by a woman, Dalkilic's lowest depth while holding her breath is an impressive 394 feet. As you might expect, the couple spends much of their time in the water. "We do around three hundred to five hundred dives a year, the average being thirty to forty-five per month," says Castineyra.

MIND, MATTER, AND MONEY OVER THE DEEP END

Popular in Europe, South America, New Zealand, the Caribbean, and the South Pacific, competitive free diving attracts daring divers who plumb dangerously deep oceans without scuba gear. The sport classifies four categories in competing for depth, and each category poses the heavy challenge of enduring intensifying atmospheric pressure and maintaining a dangerously slow heart rate. The deeper you go, the darker this dare gets; loss of consciousness before resurfacing is not uncommon.

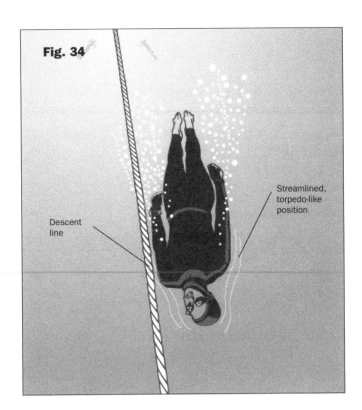

Fig. 34

Streamlined, torpedo-like position

Descent line

While some might contend that the desire to swim to extreme depths signals a troubled psyche, Castineyra says that mental health is imperative to success. "Obviously, someone with any kind of phobias or fears will not do well in free diving, where you can encounter . . . darkness, cold, claustrophobic conditions, extreme pressure, and nitrogen narcosis," among other dangers, he says.

Less contentious is the fact that free diving requires rigorous physical discipline. The muscles need to perform grueling tasks without oxygen, which requires tremendous strength and constant practice. "Muscles should be strong but not big," Castineyra adds, "since larger muscles consume more oxygen. It is a very delicate and rigorous regime to follow. The usual training period before trying to set a record is about six months, five to six days per week, three to four hours per day." A training regimen for free diving should include swimming, cycling, running, rowing, calisthenics, and a weight-bearing exercise for the arms.

In addition to training, the sport demands compliance with rather costly conventions of safety. "To do free diving safely is important, difficult, and very expensive," says Castineyra. "Basically, an accident can happen to anybody, at any time, during any dive, anywhere." Due to the danger, a dive requires a big support team of scuba divers, many of whom require special gear. Also, the performance (for a record attempt) must be filmed and documented underwater, requiring another team of camera operators and photographers. And then there are the big boats necessary to carry these huge teams, dive gear, facilities, special gases such as helium for the safety of divers going below 200 feet, resuscitation equipment, and doctors. A properly organized record attempt can cost anywhere between $85,000 and $150,000—most of it dedicated to safety! For most of us, the cost alone is prohibitive.

Yet, with all the mental, physical, and financial tolls that free diving takes, Castineyra articulates the profound lure that keeps drawing people like him and his wife into the deep. "The thrill of free diving," he says, "is accomplishing something that is, from an evolutionary point of view, negated to us—to roam freely in the sea with nothing more than our own skill and wisdom. The communion of the diver with the sea, the silence and awe and the 'revelations' you feel down there are hard to explain, but that's what it is in the end: a way to dig deep within yourself and find great peace and beauty. The moment you go down, everything changes. You feel you are in another world, another time even, and another set of behaviors and patterns takes over. You are no longer a land creature. Underwater, you are truly weightless and free, something you can't do with scuba tanks. Only free divers get that feeling."

SANE PEOPLE
KEEP RIGHT
OF THIS STUNT

HOW THE DAREDEVIL DOES IT

Checklist: calm, deep body of water; boat; descent line with depth tags; well-trained support team; oxygen supply; heart monitors; ropes; long-blade free-diving fins/or mono-fin; low-volume mask and snorkel; semi-dry suit or thick wet suit with a hood; gloves and bootees; free-diving computer/or basic scuba-diving computer

1. Perform several warm-up dives to shallow depths of between fifty and eighty feet with no air in the lungs, which will compress the lungs and simulate pressure at greater depths.

2. While on the boat, conduct a series of breathing exercises (about five to eight minutes each) in which you fill your lungs with air, which feeds oxygen to the lungs and equalizes the ears. To oxygenate the body properly, fill your lungs with air and hold your breath for forty seconds, then slowly exhale.

3. About twenty times or so, repeat step 2, taking as long as two or more hours to prepare yourself for the dive.

4. Put on your dive gear. Have safety team members stationed at intervals of thirty to fifty feet along the descent line. (The descent line is a nylon rope affixed with weights to anchor it to the bottom of the sea. It is placed there by dive officials or the diver's support team prior to a dive attempt, and anchored on the surface to a boat or a buoy.)

5. Following a final breathing cycle, fill your lungs and dive.

6. Swim alongside the line until you are between fifty and sixty feet below the water's surface, at which point you will become negatively buoyant.

7. Streamline your posture into a torpedolike pose and free-fall headfirst to the bottom (see Fig. 34).

8. At the bottom of your dive, retrieve the depth tag used in competition, which will be placed at a prede-termined depth. (The depth tag is set up by dive offi-cials and is attached to the descent line. The dis-tance at which the tag is placed has been premea-sured on land.)

9. After retrieving the tag, start your ascent and swim up to the surface, which will be significantly more difficult with the negative buoyancy now working against you.

10. Deliver the tag to a judge at the surface, rest on the boat, and inhale pure oxygen for ten to fifteen min-utes to restore yourself.

DANGER: Eardrums can rupture or collapse on a deep dive. Also, free divers are likely to suffer potentially life-threatening blackouts toward the end of their dives due to lack of oxygen.

Chapter 35

DIVING FROM TWENTY-NINE FEET INTO TWELVE INCHES OF WATER

Danny "Cosmo" Higginbottom picked up his nickname while working as a professional high diver in Hong Kong. Chinese audience members remarked that he seemed as if he had come from out of this world, that he was somehow a cosmic figure. The slim and trim Cosmo (five feet ten inches, 150 pounds) is a professional diver and stuntman whose résumé includes appearances in films such as *The Basketball Diaries* and *Monster's Ball,* and on TV shows such as *The Tonight Show with Jay Leno* and Steve Harvey's *Big Time Show.*

COSMIC SWAN FLOP

High diving into any depth of water is an impressive feat. High diving into impossibly shallow depths is an art reserved for a select few stunt professionals. It is extremely dangerous and you have to know exactly what you are doing before taking the plunge: It is as much a test of a person's faith in his skills as it is a test of the skills themselves.

Cosmo holds the world record for performing the highest shallow dive: In January 2004, he broke his own previous record by performing a controlled belly flop from a height of twenty-nine feet three inches into a depth of only twelve inches of water in a small backyard inflatable pool.

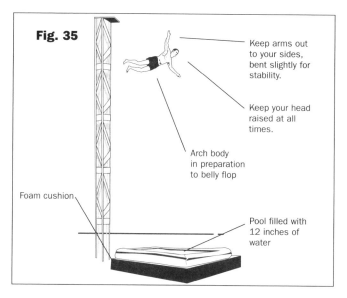

Fig. 35

Keep arms out to your sides, bent slightly for stability.

Keep your head raised at all times.

Arch body in preparation to belly flop

Foam cushion

Pool filled with 12 inches of water

For most of us, this record is hard to believe. For those who know Cosmo, it is yet another feather in his fear-less-diving cap. Diving and stunting are in the forty-two-year-old's blood. In 1972, at the age of ten, Cosmo, who was ranked in the top three in Louisiana in his age group for diving, went with his dad to see a stuntman perform a high fall onto an air bag in their hometown of Metairie. The stuntman, the late Dar Robinson, was testing an air bag for a local company. After seeing Robinson do his high fall from about fifty or sixty feet, the young Cosmo looked at his father and said, "That's what I'm going to do when I grow up!" His father replied, "You can do whatever you want if you put your mind to it and work hard at it."

For the past twenty years, Cosmo has worked hard and his father's words, like a prophecy, have come true. He has worked throughout the world as a professional diver. He took home the bronze from the finals of the 1994 World High Diving Championships, and he made his entrée into the stuntman biz when he doubled for Leonardo DiCaprio in the movie *The Basketball Diaries,* leaping off a cliff into the Hudson River.

Cosmo first left his mark in The *Guinness Book of World Records* when he achieved the world's "highest shallow dive" in 1999. He executed a controlled belly flop from twenty-nine feet into just twelve inches of water. "When I hit the water," Cosmo says, "the water hits the sides of the pool, and is then instantaneously sucked back toward me, acting somewhat as a cushioning wave."

Of course, the cushion is far from comfy. When he is hitting the water at thirty miles per hour, pain—and his ability to endure it—becomes an inevitable component of performing the stunt. Cosmo says, "I imagine it's as if I were decked out in football gear, just standing around, and a professional NFL linebacker comes running at me full speed and knocks the crap out of me."

Remarkably, in his many performances Cosmo has never been seriously injured. Once, he suffered a contusion to his knee, which swelled to the size of a cabbage; and, on the day he set his most recent record in Germany, he dislocated a shoulder. But Cosmo was quick to recover—and is an enthusiastic and focused performer. "Fear is natural," he says. "You get in trouble when you lose your sense of fear. I just try to channel my fear into positive energy."

HOW THE DAREDEVIL DOES IT

These instructions are for reading entertainment only. They are not to be followed, nor do they convey the full extent of knowledge and training required to attempt these dangerous acts.

Checklist: inflatable pool that measures six feet wide and twelve feet long and at least eighteen inches deep; ten-inch-deep foam cushion that measures six feet wide and twelve feet long; sturdy, level platform

1. Practice diving and falling from varying heights into water. This so-called high dive is really more of a belly flop, but you should become experienced in all manner of falling into water.

2. When you feel skilled enough to attempt the twenty-nine-foot dive, set up your platform. Drop a line straight down from the edge of the platform to the ground.

3. Where the line hits the ground, measure between five and seven feet forward. Place the foam cushion so the pad extends another six feet out and cover it with the inflatable pool.

4. Make sure the pad and pool are completely level, and fill the pool with twelve inches of water.

5. Climb up to your platform and stand at the edge. Curl your toes around the edge of the platform and squat down with your rear end on your haunches.

6. While holding on to the platform, lean forward over its edge, push your legs up, but not too abruptly, and exhale: do not hold your breath, as that will cause you to tense your body and increase your chances of injury upon landing.

7. The thrust of pushing your legs up (not too forcefully or you'll overshoot your target) should launch you into a parachute fall position. Your body should be arched, with your arms out to the side, bent at the elbows, for stability. At this point, you aren't really diving, but executing a controlled belly flop straight down. (see Fig. 35).

8. Keep your head up at all times as you fall, but as you glimpse the water approaching below you, put your hands out slightly in front of your body.

9. When your hands touch the water, let them bounce off as you arch your body and brace for impact. Do not bend your arms or knees forward.

10. Step out of the pool and take a bow.

DANGER: While performing this stunt, if your landing is anything but perfect, you can easily break your neck or other bones, crack your skull open, or die.

Chapter 36

FLIPPING FORWARD IN MIDAIR AND SLAM-DUNKING A BASKETBALL

Jerry L. Burrell is a professional "acrodunker"— that is, he combines the art of the slam dunk with trampoline-assisted acrobatics—and makes a nice living doing so. For ten years, from 1993 to 2003, Burrell played the part of Turbo, entertaining fans of the NBA's Houston Rockets.

AIR TURBO

Basketball is one of the most popular sports on the planet. Acrobatics is not. Combine the two, however, and you have the makings of a great National Basketball Association mascot, an extremely talented athlete, and an agile and skilled daredevil—more outrageous than the Harlem Globetrotters, more spectacular than the Ice Capades.

"I'd been doing flips and things ever since I was a kid. I was a gymnast in college, at Arizona State, and I competed. The coach took us around to do shows and things, and I just loved it. After college, I entered the workforce and didn't like it, and so I set out on a mission to find something I loved. When the Rockets audition came up in 1993, I flew myself out to Houston, and I wound up getting the job."

Today, the thirty-nine-year-old leads the Houston-based High Impact Squad—a group of six acrobats and

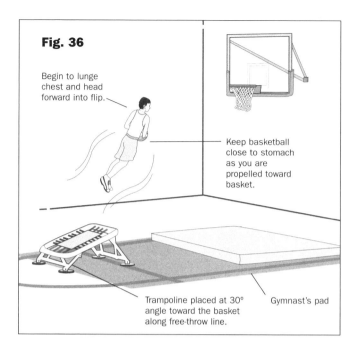

Fig. 36

Begin to lunge chest and head forward into flip.

Keep basketball close to stomach as you are propelled toward basket.

Trampoline placed at 30° angle toward the basket along free-throw line.

Gymnast's pad

gymnasts who travel around doing halftime shows for the NBA and performing inspirational shows for young people. Clad in a flashy, spandex superhero getup, complete with mask, Burrell is considered the premier acrobatic slam-dunker in the world.

But Burrell is by no means arrogant about his superhero dunking abilities; he knows that it's what he does just before the dunk that makes him so well regarded. "Almost anyone can dunk the ball once they've hit the trampoline," Burrell says, "but it is what you do from the time you hit the trampoline until you dunk the ball that is important. What makes acrodunking so dynamic is what you do while you are in the air. Flying through the air affords the opportunity to create some flair."

If that's the case, then the forward-flip slam dunk has flair to spare. It is one of Burrell's more dangerous stunts. Holding a basketball, he bounces off the trampoline and does a forward flip in the air. He then leans his body forward until it is horizontal, rotating more until his head is pointing to the floor, and then all the way around until his body is upright again. At this point, he slam-dunks the ball, clings to the rim, and drops to the floor. "This is difficult," he says, "because at some point your back is to the rim and the backboard, and if you have timed it wrong, that is, if you've been too aggressive on the jump off the trampoline, you can smash into the backboard and hurt yourself."

Success in performing this stunt depends on how fast and how hard you hit the trampoline. It also depends on the angle of the trampoline. The trampoline Burrell uses has longer legs closer to the basket and shorter legs on the other side, so the approaching daredevil is hitting a trampoline poised at a thirty-degree angle toward the basket.

"The front-flip dunk is probably the riskiest, but once you learn it, it is not so difficult. It involves the fear factor, which comes in when you have your back turned to the net and backboard," Burrell says. "You are turning your back to the goal and waiting until your head comes back around."

CROSSING AHEAD
TO INSANITY

The fear factor tends to make first-timers a little hesitant. "The first time a guy does a front-flip dunk," Burrell says, "he may underestimate it. He knows there is something in front of him, and he wants to dunk the ball, but he lands short. He approaches it with caution. But after some trial and error, you get more aggressive, and you hit the trampoline a little harder and you adjust and then you get it, and then you do a bunch of them and you get to the point where you can almost do them blindfolded."

HOW THE DAREDEVIL DOES IT

These instructions are for reading entertainment only. They are not to be followed, nor do they convey the full extent of knowledge and training required to attempt these dangerous acts.

Checklist: regulation NBA basketball; ten-foot-high basket; square trampoline, measuring twelve inches to twenty-four inches, set at a thirty-degree angle toward the basket; regulation-marked basketball court; gymnast's pad; light clothing

1. Place the front edge of the trampoline along the free-throw line so that the higher side of it faces the basket. Place the gymnast's pad in front of the basket to cushion your landing.

2. Line up at the opposite free-throw line, then start running toward the trampoline with the basketball in your hands.

3. Leap high into the air, come down onto the trampoline with both feet, and propel yourself toward the basket.

4. As you are launched toward the basket, propel your straightened body into a forward revolution by lunging your chest and head forward. Keep the ball close to your stomach (see Fig. 36).

5. Continue to rotate, with body straightened, through one full revolution.

6. As you begin to feel the completion of your flip, extend your arms out in front of you.

7. If you have timed the flip properly, you should be ready for the dunk when your body faces the basket again. Slam the ball through the hoop and hang onto the rim momentarily before dropping to the floor.

DANGER: If you launch yourself too strongly, you could end up with a forehead full of metal rim; if you launch yourself too weakly, you could end up with a face full of floor.

Chapter 37

POGO-STICK JUMPING IN THE AMAZON RIVER

With a few friends in tow and a pogo stick ready for action, Ashrita Furman embarked on his journey into the heart of darkness in the late 1980s. The fifty-year-old is a true pioneer of Guinness world records. When he's not managing his health food store in Jamaica, New York, he is setting scores of records for various notable feats such as balancing the most number of pint glasses on his chin (see page 68). In 1987, he was the proud recipient of a title for the most Guinness records set in different categories.

BOUNCING INTO THE HEART OF DARKNESS

Amazon. The name itself conjures up images of venomous snakes, gigantic women, and evil deeds executed and quickly hidden under the cover of jungle darkness. Indeed, the Amazon is a wild and dangerous place. The world's second longest river, the Amazon wends across the width of South America just south of the equator, a haven to the enormous anaconda and the ferocious piranha, which uses its razor-sharp teeth to eat live prey. It is just the place for an adventurous pogo-stick-wielding daredevil to make a brave and bouncy stand.

It was the same year he set off to South America to break his previous record of pogo-sticking underwater for three hours and twenty minutes. "I first set the record of three hours and twenty minutes in a neighborhood YMCA pool, but while on vacation in South America, I got inspired to surpass the record in the Amazon River," Furman says.

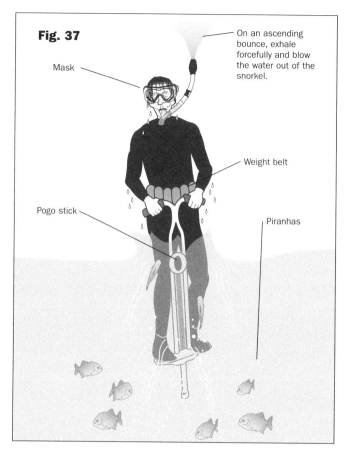

Fig. 37

Mask

On an ascending bounce, exhale forcefully and blow the water out of the snorkel.

Weight belt

Pogo stick

Piranhas

Furman and a few close friends flew into the interior of Peru, where they boarded a speedboat and proceeded deep into the rain forest. "It began storming and it got dark," Furman remembers. "We stayed overnight in a small village."

The next morning, Furman and company, along with a knowledgeable guide, journeyed in a wooden dugout canoe down a tributary of the Amazon, where the canopy of vines grew increasingly dense overhead. "Then we found a spot in the middle of nowhere," Furman says. "The spot had the depth I was looking for, between eight and ten feet. I asked the guide if the location had any piranhas, but he just laughed and pointed to the black water fifty feet away. That was not the reply I was hoping to get."

Undaunted, Furman entered the murky water with his pogo stick in hand, a mask and snorkel on his face, and ten pounds of scuba weights and a rope harnessed around his waist for his crew on shore to hang on to, should he get into any serious trouble. "I later found out that if the man-eating fish did attack, by the time I got reeled in, all [that my crew] would find would be the pogo stick!" A piranha feeding frenzy usually leaves behind only clouds of red in the water; Furman was lucky not to have become prey.

He was not so lucky at first with the thick, muddy river bottom. "I didn't realize the bottom of the Amazon is composed of a thick clay, so I got stuck several times at first, and almost lost my pogo stick. I didn't want to let go of it when it got stuck. So there I was, tugging at it underwater, trying to get it out of the mud, while my friends are trying to yank me out of the water, thinking I'm getting eaten alive."

After resolving the technical difficulties, Furman found more solid ground along a patchwork of submerged tree roots. For the next three hours, Furman bounced along to the heartbeat of the jungle: exhaling and blowing water out of his snorkel as he emerged above the waterline, quickly inhaling before sinking back to the bottom.

Furman kept a steady pace, until a black water snake wrapped itself around his leg. "Having never encountered a jumping animal like me before, I presume it got frightened, because it quickly let go," he says. Totally freaked out, Furman tore off his mask and snorkel, but the serpent was gone as quickly as it appeared. He continued on with his stunt, but the snake certainly symbolized the lurking dangers. Nonetheless, in that single instant, Furman understood the sinister power of his surroundings. His instinct echoed, momentarily, those final notorious words of dying adventurer Kurtz in Joseph Conrad's *Heart of Darkness*. "The horror, the horror." But unlike Kurtz, he lives to tell.

HOW THE DAREDEVIL DOES IT:

These instructions are for reading entertainment only. They are not to be followed, nor do they convey the full extent of knowledge and training required to attempt these dangerous acts.

Checklist: pogo stick; mask and snorkel; ten-pound weighted scuba belt; level surface at a depth of eight to ten feet in the world's second longest river

1. Wearing the mask, snorkel, and weight belt, swim to the desired spot in the Amazon River, with your pogo stick in hand.

2. Take a deep breath of air through the snorkel above the water's surface and let yourself sink.

3. At the bottom, bounce yourself back up to the water's surface.

4. As your head breaks the water's surface, blow the air out of your lungs and the water out of your snorkel (see Fig. 37).

5. Inhale quickly and deeply before sinking back below the surface.

6. Repeat for three hours, or until latest record is broken.

DANGER: The danger is not so much in the stunt as it is in the setting: There are many dangerous life-forms lurking in the murky depths of the Amazon.

Chapter 38

BECOMING A HUMAN CANNONBALL

If where we are from says anything about us as individuals, Dave Smith Sr.'s hometown—Halfway, Missouri—was a strange forecast of things to come. By the time he was twenty-seven, Smith's career interests were divided between teaching math to grammar-school kids and developing the flair for gymnastics he had discovered while in college. After an old college buddy came through town performing a trapeze act with a circus in the late 1960s, there was no more half way about it. Smith packed his wife, two small children, and some of their possessions into the car and joined the circus.

FATHER KNOWS BLAST

The human cannonball feat has graced the modern circus and amusement arena for more than 125 years. William Hunt—also known as The Great Farini—is often considered the father of human cannonballing. On April 2, 1877, Farini launched the first human, a fourteen-year-old girl named Zazel, from the shaft of a cannon into flight. Five years later, Farini and Zazel became stars in P. T. Barnum's Greatest Show on Earth.

"It was a fluke thing," he says. "My buddy called and said he was coming through town. I went to see the show, and eight days later I was packed up and ready to leave."

Smith spent his first five years in the circus as a catcher for the trapeze act. Looking for an act that he could do by himself, Smith became interested in doing the human cannonball. He spent nights awake thinking about how

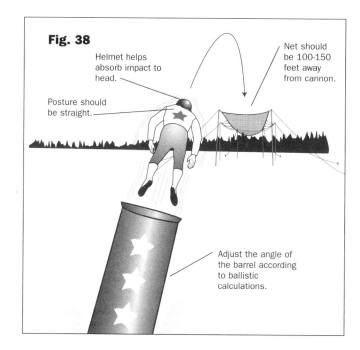

Fig. 38

Helmet helps absorb impact to head.

Posture should be straight.

Net should be 100-150 feet away from cannon.

Adjust the angle of the barrel according to ballistic calculations.

he could build a cannon. Conveniently, he was a tinkerer who liked to build things himself. After a few years of building and tweaking cannon prototypes, Smith perfected the design for a cannon and took his stunt on the road.

Cannons used to fire humans do not use gunpowder. Most are either spring-activated or air-compressed. But Smith won't say what propulsion system he uses; that's his trade secret. He won't even let fans and spectators get too close to the cannon because he doesn't want them to see how the stunt is done. For entertainment value, fireworks are often used to create the sound of a cannon blast.

Altogether, Smith has built seven cannons. He used to weave his own nets, but has since stopped doing so because the type of rope he needs is no longer available. The net is, of course, even more important than the cannon. The net must be strong so it can bring to an abrupt stop a 150- to 160-pound man flying through the air.

Smith is usually going around sixty miles per hour when he leaves the cannon, and is only in the air for about three or four seconds before landing on the net. He has no directional control over his body once he's in the air, and thus, if the cannon has not been properly aimed, he can die on impact if he heads for something other than the net. In addition, G forces can be between 7 and 10 when he is shot out of the cannon, elevating the danger level even further. (A G force of 7 means the body is subjected to seven times the pressure it is normally under when standing still.)

Smith has been blasted over a one-hundred-foot-tall Ferris wheel, over small buildings, and has even performed in a "dueling cannons" event with his son, Dave Smith Jr., who is also an accomplished human cannonball. Both men have done thousands of cannon shots. Dad holds the world record for the longest cannon flight at 185 feet 10 inches, while his son's longest is a mere yard and a half shorter. So what does Smith junior think of while he's flying through the air at sixty miles per hour? "I some-times think about getting a new job," he says.

But he amends his statement: "When you have a huge crowd around you, it is just the opposite. I can see indi-vidual faces through the crowd. I can see their eyes. The little kids think you're Superman. It is often very peace-ful in the air."

HOW THE DAREDEVIL DOES IT

These instructions are for reading entertainment only. They are not to be followed, nor do they convey the full extent of knowledge and training required to attempt these dangerous acts.

Checklist: spring-activated or air-compressed cannon; strong net; trusty assistant; helmet; tight-fitting clothes to minimize wind drag

1. Set up a reliable spring-activated or air-compressed cannon.

2. Set up a strong net about 100 to 150 feet away from the cannon. The net should be parallel to the ground, covering a significant amount of target area.

3. Consider the three primary factors in determining a ballistic flight path: cannon angle, gravity, and speed. You will need a basic knowledge of science and physics to factor in other variables such as your weight, wind and air pressure, your resistance to air and wind pressure, and the tricky aerodynamics of a human body that has little control over its positioning.

4. Adjust the angle of the barrel of the cannon according to your calculations so that you will land on the net.

5. Test your cannon with something that resembles your body's weight and shape, like a long bag of sand, and make adjustments as necessary.

6. Strap on your helmet and climb inside the barrel of the cannon.

7. While inside the cannon, keep your legs extended and body straight. When you are ready, have your assistant release the firing mechanism on the cannon.

8. G forces will compress your body slightly as you leave the cannon. As you fly through the air, there is very little you can do to control your flight path, and you won't have any control over your limbs. But try to maintain a straight, rigid posture (see Fig. 38).

9. If the cannon was aimed properly, you should land safely on the net. Ideally, you will be able to twist around during your descent so that you land on your back.

DANGER: Many notable cannonballers have had their careers cut short because of broken necks and broken backs. Many uncontrollable variables play into the physics of trajectory, and more than one daredevil has paid the ultimate price due to this unpredictability.

Chapter 39

PARACHUTING OFF A BUILDING

Thirty-three-year-old Jason Bell has been jumping off buildings and bridges for over a decade. He is an avid BASE jumping enthusiast and owns a company in West Virginia, Vertical Visions, that is dedicated to sharing information and resources related to the extreme sport.

SKYSCRAPER SKYDIVING

It's a bird! It's a plane! No, it's a daredevil! Skyscraper skydiving is an extremely dangerous, often illegal, and sometimes fatal recreation of choice for an underground group of thrill seekers associated with a sport called BASE jumping. This high-adrenaline pastime is the art of parachuting from fixed objects as opposed to jumping out of airplanes. BASE is an acronym for building, antennae, span, and earth, referring to the various kinds of fixed platforms from which BASE daredevils jump. These range from bridges, cliffs, and, perhaps most dangerous of all, skyscrapers.

The short distances involved in BASE jumping means the daredevil has only 3.5 to 5 seconds to pull open his parachute. Most BASE jumpers are experienced skydivers, with as many as 100 to 150 skydiving jumps under their belts before they attempt a BASE jump.

Besides the fact that BASE jumpers take off from much lower elevations than regular skydivers, there are two key differences between skydiving and BASE jumping that make the latter sport considerably more dangerous. One is that skydivers today use two chutes—the main one and an emergency backup. They are also equipped with an automated chute activation system that senses air

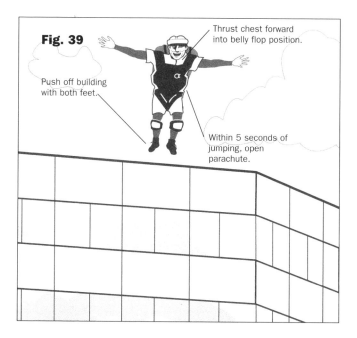

Fig. 39

Thrust chest forward into belly flop position.

Push off building with both feet.

Within 5 seconds of jumping, open parachute.

pressure and speed and automatically opens a chute if the jumper fails to do so manually. BASE jumpers don't use any of those safety backup systems.

The other major hazard is the potential for crashing into the building from which the jump is executed. Many BASE jumpers have died over the years as a result of just this. When jumping off bridges and cliffs, winds cannot be more than fifteen miles per hour. To jump off a building, winds must be no greater than five miles per hour.

But for Bell, there is an undeniable thrill to jumping off buildings and bridges: "This is basically extreme skydiving. Most people who do it are looking for that next level of extreme sport experience, the stomach-in-the-mouth feeling.

"Buildings are dangerous because, typically, the winds are strange in big cities. You have to measure your winds. I will jump off buildings only when the wind is five miles or less. Jumping off a building is the strangest of all BASE jumps because you get up there and stand on the edge and you don't feel like you belong on the edge of a building. People will think that I'm a suicide jumper. It is also difficult because your landing area is small. You're landing on 47th Avenue and are dodging taxis and buses and cars," Bell says.

There is also the legal aspect: some building owners don't want BASE jumpers using their buildings, so jumpers must have permission to jump, or must do it on the sly.

"Every time, I still get scared when I do it," Bell says.

BASE jumpers typically use larger chutes than skydivers, which help them to slow down more quickly in the narrower time frame. Bell says that when he lands, he is traveling no faster than if he had jumped off a dining-room chair. But a lot of expertise goes into a jump to ensure a safe landing, and even the most experienced jumpers risk their lives each time they step off a building. The sport has claimed many lives already; many BASE enthusiasts adamantly oppose newcomers adopting the recreation casually.

As Ronald "Slim" Simpson, the Australian jumper who organizes the world championships at the Petronas Twin Towers in Kuala Lumpur, Malaysia, likes to say: "There is no step-by-step for BASE. There is one step and you better know what you're doing before you take it."

HOW THE DAREDEVIL DOES IT

These instructions are for reading entertainment only. They are not to be followed, nor do they convey the full extent of knowledge and training required to attempt these dangerous acts.

Checklist: large high-quality parachute; tall building; high-top shoes or boots; full-face helmet; gloves; padded motorcycle suit for extra protection

1. Plan your jump according to the weather reports. Do not jump if winds are stronger than five miles per hour

2. Find a building you want to jump from. It should be at least four hundred feet tall. Be sure to select one that has some landing space around or near it.

3. Scope out landing sites on the ground and determine the best place to land.

4. Get permission from the building's owner to jump. You'll probably have to pledge not to sue the owner if you get injured.

5. Pack up your parachute and put on all of your equipment while you're still on the ground, then take an elevator to the top of the building.

6. Stand on the building's edge, above your landing spot.

7. When you are ready, push off with both feet and thrust your chest forward, as if you were belly flopping into a swimming pool (see Fig. 39). Your body should be horizontal and parallel to the ground. You want to be facing away from the building.

8. Within three to five seconds of jumping, pull open your parachute. Steer your open parachute by pulling on the cords attached to your body harnes. Tug at the right cord to veer right, on the left cord to veer left.

9. Aim toward your landing spot and fall gently to the ground upon landing.

DANGER: BASE jumping is an extremely risky pursuit that can prove fatal for even experienced jumpers. It should not be undertaken lightly, if at all.

BIBLIOGRAPHY

Books

Taylor, James and Kothcer, Kathleen. *James Taylor's Shocked & Amazed: On & Off the Midway.* Connecticut: The Lyons Press, 2002.

Menzel, Peter and D'Aluisio, Faith. *Man Eating Bugs: The Art and Science of Eating Insects.* Berkeley: Ten Speed Press, 1998.

Radio Transcript

Foreign Correspondent: "Japan - Food Fight" Broadcast: August 14, 2002; Reporter: Mark Simkin.

ABOUT THE AUTHOR

Ben Ikenson is a writer of speeches and articles that range in subject from wildlife conservation to wild road trips. His work has appeared in numerous nature and travel magazines and newspaper travel sections. He has contributed to several books and is the author of *PATENTS: Ingenious Inventions: How They Work and How They Came to Be.* He popped his first wheelie on a tricycle at age six. This early feat developed into a lifelong obsession with the art of the daredevil. He lives in Washington, DC.

An EYE book published by arrangement with Barnes & Noble, Inc.